A GLORIOUS PAST

MILESTONES IN BLACK AMERICAN HISTORY

A GLORIOUS PAST

ANCIENT EGYPT, ETHIOPIA, AND NUBIA

Earnestine Jenkins

CHELSEA HOUSE PUBLISHERS
New York   Philadelphia

FRONTISPIECE   The goddess Isis leads Queen Nofretari, wife of the pharaoh Ramses II, in a wall painting from Egypt's Valley of the Kings.

ON THE COVER   One of Egypt's most powerful rulers, Ramses II, is portrayed in stone in front of his temple at Abu Simbel in the former kingdom of Nubia.

Chelsea House Publishers
Editorial Director   Richard Rennert
Executive Managing Editor   Karyn Gullen Browne
Copy Chief   Robin James
Picture Editor   Adrian G. Allen
Art Director   Robert Mitchell
Manufacturing Director   Gerald Levine

Milestones in Black American History
Senior Editor   Marian W. Taylor
Series Originator and Adviser   Benjamin I. Cohen
Series Consultants   Clayborne Carson, Darlene Clark Hine
Series Designer   Rae Grant

Staff for A GLORIOUS PAST
Assistant Editor   Margaret Dornfeld
Editorial Assistant   Annie McDonnell
Picture Researcher   Sandy Jones

3 5 7 9 8 6 4

Library of Congress Cataloging-in-Publication Data

Jenkins, Earnestine.
    A glorious past: ancient Egypt, Ethiopia, and Nubia/Earnestine Jenkins.
      p. cm.—(Milestones in Black American history)
    Includes bibliographical references and index.
      ISBN 0-7910-2258-7
      ISBN 0-7910-2684-1 (pbk.)
    1. Egypt—History—332 B.C.—Juvenile literature. 2. Ethiopia—History—To 1400—Juvenile literature. 3. Nubia—History—Juvenile literature. I. Title. II. Series.
DT83.J46 1994   94-10713
932—dc20   CIP
                                                                        AC

	Introduction	7
	Milestones	9
1	Land of the Pharaohs	13
2	Egyptian Religion	35
3	Life in the Nile Valley	51
4	"Land of the Burnt Faces"	69
5	The Rise of Meroë	79
6	A Procession of Faiths	89
7	The Ancient Kingdom of Axum	97
	Further Reading	114
	Index	115

MILESTONES IN BLACK AMERICAN HISTORY

ANCIENT EGYPT, ETHIOPIA, AND NUBIA

THE WEST AFRICAN KINGDOMS (750-1900)

THE AGE OF DISCOVERY AND THE SLAVE TRADE

FROM THE ARRIVAL OF THE ENSLAVED AFRICANS
TO THE END OF THE AMERICAN REVOLUTION (1619–1784)

FROM THE FRAMING OF THE CONSTITUTION
TO *WALKER'S APPEAL* (1787–1829)

FROM THE NAT TURNER REVOLT
TO THE FUGITIVE SLAVE LAW (1831–1850)

FROM *UNCLE TOM'S CABIN*
TO THE ONSET OF THE CIVIL WAR (1851–1861)

FROM THE EMANCIPATION PROCLAMATION
TO THE CIVIL RIGHTS BILL OF 1875 (1863–1875)

FROM THE END OF RECONSTRUCTION
TO THE ATLANTA COMPROMISE (1877–1895)

FROM THE "SEPARATE BUT EQUAL" DOCTRINE
TO THE BIRTH OF THE NAACP (1896–1909)

FROM THE GREAT MIGRATION
TO THE HARLEM RENAISSANCE (1910–1930)

FROM THE SCOTTSBORO CASE
TO THE BREAKING OF BASEBALL'S COLOR BARRIER (1931–1947)

FROM THE DESEGREGATION OF THE ARMED FORCES
TO THE MONTGOMERY BUS BOYCOTT (1948–1956)

FROM THE FOUNDING OF THE SOUTHERN CHRISTIAN
LEADERSHIP CONFERENCE TO THE
ASSASSINATION OF MALCOLM X (1957–1965)

FROM THE SELMA-MONTGOMERY MARCH
TO THE FORMATION OF PUSH (1965–1971)

FROM THE GARY CONVENTION
TO THE PRESENT (1972–)

INTRODUCTION

The ancestors of every present-day U.S. resident came from another continent. The majority—those with European roots—often know, and take pride in knowing, a good deal about the Old World and its influence on America's birth. Few Americans, however, know as much about the other components of their nation's cultural heritage. Among the most neglected—and extraordinary—of those components are the stories of black America's early homelands and of the eras when people of color played history's leading roles.

This is a narrative that begins far, far before the dark year of 1619, when the first enslaved Africans dragged themselves ashore to begin more than two centuries of bondage in the New World. The story of ancient Africa—the rich, teeming pageants of Egypt, Nubia, and Ethiopia—makes one of the most compelling narratives in the human experience.

The saga of these vibrant African nations opens with the mighty civilization of pharaonic Egypt. Here are the royal rulers, proud kings who immortalized themselves with monuments that would proclaim their power through all recorded time. Here, too, are the people who lived on the banks of the Nile, giver of life and death to millions. Here is an intimate view of the Egyptians and their land's political system, its cities, families, arts, architecture, festivals, occupations, magic, and religion—a system of beliefs so deep and so much a part of everyday life that the Egyptians' language included no separate word for it.

From the panoply of Egypt, the narrative moves on to equally spectacular but less familiar Nubia. For centuries identified by Europeans as "Aethiopia," a Greek-rooted word meaning "land of the burnt faces," Nubia lasted for 5,000 years—longer than Greece, Rome, or ancient Egypt. By turns conquered and conquerors, the Nubians possessed unimaginable wealth in gold. They were also first-class builders, creating an astonishing number of exquisite temples and tombs, many of which remain to reflect their early glory. Adorning these structures—and their owners—were the products of Nubia's highly skilled artists: jewelry, sculpture, and pottery brilliantly wrought from the nation's gold, ebony, ivory, bronze, glass, and silver. Like the neighboring Egyptians, the Nubians developed their own alphabet, a type of shorthand so complex that modern scientists have yet to decipher it. Both Christianity and Islam left deep imprints on this land, their strength witnessed by houses of worship, murals, and other works inspired by the population's deep faith.

The "blackfaced ones" (as they were identified by the Europeans) of Ethiopia, a land originally know as Axum, also developed a complex and sophisticated society. During its 1,000-year history, Axum came to control much of northern Africa and the fabulously wealthy Red Sea trade. The nation produced a number of history's most powerful and effective rulers, including Ezana. A strong king of the 3rd century A.D., Ezana extended his country's authority over vast stretches of territory and established Christianity as his subjects' religion. In the story of the ancient world, Ezana also stands tall for his patronage of the arts, a field that blossomed phenomenally under his rule. Axumite architects created a dazzling array of monuments, many of them still erect, and its craftspeople created objects that have survived to transfix modern viewers with their beauty. Axumite literature, too, lives on, notably in the fascinating story of the queen of Sheba and her visit to Jerusalem's fabled King Solomon.

The power of these great civilizations has vanished, but their breathtaking testimony continues to awe and inspire the world.

MILESTONES
750-1900

ca. 3800 B.C. • The first Nubian culture emerges in northern Nubia, forming what may be the earliest monarchy in human history.

3100 • Menes, a ruler from Upper Egypt, conquers Lower Egypt and becomes the first pharaoh of a united Egypt.

2575–2551 • Snefru, founder of the Egyptian fourth dynasty, battles Libya, gains control of Nubia, improves foreign trade, and supports the construction of many temples and fortresses.

2551–2528 • Egyptian king Khufu spurs construction of a pyramid at Giza; the first of the Seven Wonders of the World, it remains the largest structure ever built.

2152 • The Egyptian empire falls to its eastern enemies, resulting in years of anarchy and civil war.

2061–2011 • Mentuhotep II reunites Upper and Lower Egypt, forging a strong central government at Thebes. During the Middle Kingdom era, he improves the country's irrigation system, encourages the spread of religion, and passes laws reinforcing the equality of all Egyptians.

2000 • Kerma, a city-state within Nubia, uses its successful trade with Egypt to increase its wealth, gain control of the Upper Nile, and support its flourishing craft industries.

1991–1962 • During the 12th dynasty, Amenemhet I extends Egypt's political and commercial activity into Nubia and western Asia. His eldest son, Sensuret I, builds forts along the Nile River in Nubia, setting the stage for Sensuret III to pacify the Nubians.

1652–1500 • The Hyksos, a warlike people from western Asia, conquer Lower Egypt. Besides involving Egypt in Asian events, the Hyksos strengthen the Egyptian army by introducing armor, horses, and chariots.

1580–1085 • After Ahmose liberates Egypt, he and his successors conquer the area from the Sudan to Syria, greatly augmenting Egypt's wealth and power. Pharaohs raise Nubian princes as Egyptian and then send them as viceroys to their home country.

1085 • Heri-Hor, high priest of Amon-Ra, gains control of Upper Egypt; meanwhile, Lower Egypt falls to the Libyans.

760–667 • Kashta, a Nubian leader, takes control of Egypt; his successor, Piankhi, defends the territory from the Libyans. In 716, Nubian ruler Shabaka establishes his permanent home in Egypt and spearheads a cultural and artistic revival, hiring artists to preserve important Egyptian texts and temples.

667 • The Assyrians force Nubian ruler Taharqa to leave Egypt. In 663, Ashurbanipal leads an Assyrian massacre at Thebes, completely ending Nubian rule.

654 • Egyptian prince Psammetichus overthrows the brief Assyrian rule to reunite Upper and Lower Egypt. Rulers in this period promote foreign trade, especially with Greece.

593 • After the Libyans capture Napata, the Nubians move southward, eventually settling their capital at Meroë. In relative isolation, Nubia enters a golden age of independent cultural development but continues to trade with other African states.

525 • Cambyses conquers Egypt for the Persian empire, but Egypt's culture remains distinct.

332 • Alexander the Great invades Egypt, destroying the last Egyptian dynasty.

30–28 • Rome conquers Egypt and the Dodekoschoenos, an area of the Nile Valley rich with gold mines. A few years later, Meroë battles Roman Egypt for this valuable territory, until both sign the Treaty of Samos and establish fruitful trade relations.

1st century A.D. • Nearly 1,000 years after the first Arabians arrived in northeast Africa, the Arabians and the Kushitic Africans merge their cultures into the kingdom of Axum, also known as Abyssinia.

200 • As Rome abandons the hazardous overland trade routes to Meroë in favor of the more convenient sea route to Axum, Meroë enters an economic decline.

350 • The Meroitic kingdom's distinguished reign ends when Ezana, Axum's first Christian king, invades Meroë. Axum gains control of the Red Sea trade, becoming a significant player in international trade.

450 • After doctrinal disputes at the Council of Chalcedon, Egypt and Axum separate from the Church of Rome and the Constantinople church to form the Coptic church of Egypt and the Ethiopian Orthodox church.

6th century • Nubia divides into Nobatia, Makuria, and Alwa. Despite some theological differences, the Nubians unite around the common faith of Christianity, separating the king's power from religion and managing the legal system more efficiently.

• Christianity also gains strength in Axum when King Gabre Maskal sets a precedent by giving huge land grants to the church. Church leaders eventually become powerful enough to challenge various kings' authority, and the Bible influences Axumite literature and the use of the Ge'ez language over Greek.

523 • Joseph, a prince from South Arabia (present-day Yemen), persecutes Christians who refuse to convert to Judaism. Axumite emperor Caleb defeats Joseph but never gains full control of the southern Arabian colonies. By the end of the century, as Islam spreads through Arabia and North Africa, Axum loses its premier position in the Red Sea region and northeast Africa.

641 • The Arabs take control of Egypt and then twice attempt to invade Nubia. In the face of strong Nubian resistance, the Arabs sign a treaty in 652 guaranteeing Nubian freedom for an annual tribute of slaves and the maintenance of a mosque.

8th century • After losing northern territory to Muslim nomads, Axumites conquer southern territory and reopen trade with South Arabia.

ca. 970s • Fierce attacks led by Agaw queen Judith fail to overthrow Axum but exhaust the nation's resources. The Axumites retreat to the northern mountains, and Ethiopia's center of power shifts southward.

late 14th century • After a long period of religious, political, and economic decline, the Nubian kingdoms crumble into warring principalities, and the Nubians convert to Islam.

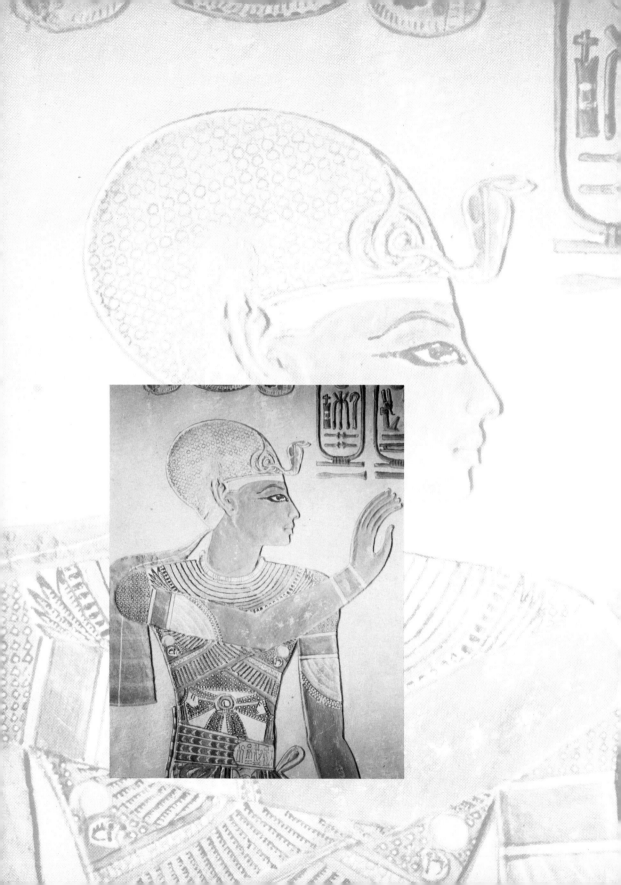

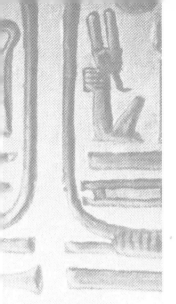

1

LAND OF THE PHARAOHS

EGYPTIAN history is said to begin around the year 3200 B.C., when Menes, a ruler from Upper Egypt, conquered Lower Egypt, merging the two kingdoms into a single empire. Menes became the first king, or pharaoh, of a united Egypt, and his descendants formed the first of Egypt's 30 dynasties.

Soon after Menes came to power, he erected a new capital at Memphis, a city on the west bank of the Nile River, about 13 miles south of Cairo, capital of present-day Egypt. The leader chose his capital well. Memphis not only straddled the border between his old and new kingdoms, offering him an important vantage point from which to control both regions, but it also lay near the spot where the Nile forked into major water routes leading north, east, and west. Menes built a series of irrigation canals that turned the marshlands surrounding Memphis into flourishing fields, and the city itself into a center of wealth and commerce. By the end of Menes' reign, Memphis had become the heart and soul of Egypt.

A portrait of Ramses III, an ambitious and effective military leader who ruled Egypt from 1190 to 1158 B.C., adorns the walls of a tomb in the Valley of the Queens.

This slate relief dates from around the 35th century B.C., some 400 years before the reign of the first Egyptian pharaohs. The bull is believed to represent a king defeating an enemy.

For many years, the Egyptians called their capital Ineb-Hedj, which meant "white wall," after the white-washed mud-brick walls of Menes' palace. Much later, during the 18th dynasty, they started to refer to the city as Men-Nefer, meaning "the enduring and beautiful pyramid of Pepy." (King Pepy I was a sixth-dynasty pharaoh who built a small pyramid at Saqqara, a village a few miles northwest of the center of Memphis.) The name *Memphis* was the Greek version of Men-Nefer. The city, an important religious site, was often called Hekaptah, meaning "the palace of the soul of Ptah." (Ptah, the patron god of Memphis, was a major divinity in the Egyptian pantheon, signifying life, sovereignty, and stability.) The Greek version of Hekaptah was *Aiegyptos*, from which the name *Egypt* is derived. *KMT*, which translates into "people of the black land," was the term the Egyptians used for themselves.

The period from 2780 to 2258 B.C., in which Egypt was ruled by the third through the sixth dynasties, is known as the Old Kingdom. The third dynasty was founded by King Djoser, a strong and innovative leader. During his reign, the world's first large-scale stone monument was built in the village of Saqqara. Known as the stepped pyramid of Djoser, this tomb was apparently designed by the royal architect, Imhotep, a gifted individual who also served as a court physician, writer, magician, and priest. Imhotep's fame was great in the ancient world, and the Greeks would later identify him with their god of medicine, Askelepios.

The fourth dynasty (2680-2565 B.C.) ushered in one of the greatest eras of the Old Kingdom. Snefru, its founder, who reigned for 24 years, won renown as a military leader. He fought successful campaigns against both the Libyans, who lived in the desert west of Memphis, and the Nubians, whose kingdom lay to the south. Snefru boasted of capturing 7,000 Nubians and 11,000 Libyans during these expeditions. Meanwhile, the king promoted trade relations with other neighboring countries, and Egypt began importing wood from Phoenicia and copper from the Sinai Peninsula during his reign. In addition to his military and economic achievements, Snefru sponsored the con-

The stepped pyramid of Djoser towers above the desert at Saqqara, a village northwest of Memphis. Built by King Djoser's royal architect, Imhotep, this temple was the first large-scale monument ever constructed of stone.

struction of numerous temples and fortresses, as well as two pyramids, both at Dashur. One of these, the so-called bent pyramid, is well known for its asymmetrical design.

The fourth-dynasty kings Khufu, Khafra, and Menkhare, who followed Snefru, are known chiefly for the three magnificent pyramids they erected at Giza. Khufu's pyramid remains the largest structure

ever built by man, and the Greeks placed it first among the Seven Wonders of the World. Later kings in Egyptian history would build exceptional tombs, but none that compared to the Giza pyramids. It is possible that the pharaohs were never able to amass the time and resources to replicate them, for clearly their construction required great sacrifice on the part of the Egyptian people.

Commissioned by the fourth-dynasty rulers Khufu, Khafra, and Menkhare, the great pyramids of Giza have awed Egypt's visitors for centuries. The largest of these tombs, the pyramid of Khufu, measures 481 feet in height and covers an area of 13 acres.

The fifth-dynasty pharaohs allied themselves with the powerful priests whose seat was at Heliopolis, some 25 miles north of Memphis. Heliopolis, which meant "City of the Sun" in Greek, was considered the sacred city of the sun god, Ra. Many of the pharaohs of the fifth dynasty had their tombs ornamented at the top by an obelisk, a four-sided pillar that tapered upward, in honor of the sun god. These tombs were smaller than the pyramids at Giza, but many of them were more elaborately ornamented. For example, inside the pyramid of the final fifth-dynasty ruler, Unis, the walls were beautifully inscribed with passages from the religious books of the Egyptians.

The pharaohs of the fifth dynasty also directed their efforts toward protecting their frontiers and encouraging the growth of trade with other countries. They fought against the Libyans, imported cedarwood from Syria, and sent a trading expedition for incense and other exotic goods to Punt, a land that historians believe may have been located in what is now Somalia.

Two outstanding pharaohs dominated the sixth dynasty (2420-2258 B.C.): Pepy I and his son, Pepy II. Pepy I sent his mighty army out to fight the nomadic peoples who lived in northeast Egypt and may have driven them back as far as Palestine. Pepy II ascended the throne when he was a child of six and ruled for 94 years; his was the longest reign in Egyptian history.

Pepy II spent much of his energy trying to annex Nubia. He mounted four expeditions to the country, bringing back ebony, oils, incense, elephant tusks, and other items from the interior of Africa. The second half of his reign was shadowed by political upheaval. At a time when the royal coffers were diminishing, Egypt's nobility and priests began demanding more privileges and land. Before long, the pharaoh was struggling to keep an army large enough to defend Egypt's borders. Lower Egypt remained especially weak and open to invasion. After the death of Pepy II, the empire fell to its eastern enemies and experienced a state of anarchy for nearly 300 years.

Historians refer to Egypt's eras of political, cultural, and economic breakdown as the intermediate periods. During these times, foreign rulers sat upon Egypt's throne. Civil war and anarchy prevailed, as local princes battled one another all along the Nile Valley. Much of what historians know about the

This 12th-dynasty wooden model shows an Egyptian supply ship manned by Canaanites, a Semitic people from Palestine. From around 2000 to 1785 B.C., Egypt's political and commercial power continued to expand; one consequence of this growth was the induction of foreigners into the Egyptian workforce.

intermediate periods is drawn from a long text by Ipu-wer called *Admonitions of a Sage.* Ipu-wer offers a vivid description of the social chaos of the First Intermediate Period (2258-2052 B.C.) and the subsequent periods of upheaval.

For decades, according to Ipu-wer, Egypt went virtually ungoverned, and turmoil spread across the country. Farmers would carry shields as they worked their land, for fear of passing marauders. Raiding armies might prevent them

from planting their crops altogether; what was already planted would rot in the fields while their livestock roamed wild. Peasants flocked to the towns in search of food and shelter, but, because trade had been disrupted, even in the cities they could not always find what they needed. Wood, for example, became so scarce that people no longer made coffins to bury their dead, but simply threw the bodies into the Nile.

Even in the midst of this chaos, however, at

Queen Hatshepsut, who became pharaoh in 1489 B.C., is perhaps best known for the magnificent architecture erected during her reign. Her mortuary temple at Deir-el-Bahri features a series of broad terraces that recede into the cliffs behind it.

Hiracleopolis in Middle Egypt (the northern part of Upper Egypt), and at Thebes in Upper Egypt, two strong seats of power were emerging. From 2154 to 2052 B.C., the Egyptian kings of the 9th and 10th dynasties ruled the Nile Delta and revived the Memphite traditions. Upper Egypt had broken up into its original provinces, called nomes, with each ruled by a local prince. By 2134 B.C., however, a dynasty centered at Thebes had begun to gain control of this region, and soon its rulers conquered the entire country. This was the advent of Egypt's Middle Kingdom (2134-1786 B.C.), the next great era of national achievement.

The pharaoh Mentuhotep II ended the civil wars by reuniting Upper and Lower Egypt. Mentuhotep reorganized the government, creating a strong, centralized administration at Thebes. He and other Middle Kingdom pharaohs also made important changes in Egypt's judicial system, passing legislation that emphasized the equality of all Egyptians before the law. Mentuhotep increased the nation's water supply by repairing and expanding the irrigation system. He also encouraged religious growth, promoting the local god of Thebes, Amon-Ra, as the national deity. At the same time, the cult of Osiris, the god of resurrection, grew more popular among Egyptians of every class; this development helped Egypt become more democratic, for Osiris held out the promise of salvation to everyone, from the pharaoh to the common man.

Amenemhet I founded the 12th dynasty (1991-1786 B.C.), a vigorous family of rulers who helped make Egypt's political base even more secure. The rulers of the 12th dynasty expanded Egypt's political and commercial activity into Nubia and western Asia. Amenemhet I initiated a policy that made the pharaoh's eldest son co-regent to the throne. This custom ensured the presence of a watchful ruler to oversee domestic affairs when the pharaoh was absent from Egypt with his armed forces, and it was continued by succeeding pharaohs. By thus entrusting the government to his son, Sensuret I, Amenemhet I was able to move his forces into Nubia.

During his own reign, Sensuret I led his army farther into Nubia than any previous pharaoh had traveled, extending his reach to the Nile River's Second Cataract (one of the Nile's series of rapids). A chain of six fortresses, begun by Sensuret I to protect Egyptian interests along the Nile, was completed by a later pharaoh, Sensuret III. Troops, armed with lances, arrows, and knives, were garrisoned at the forts, and the Nubians could not pass north of the

Second Cataract without the permission of the Egyptian fortress commander who was posted there. Sensuret III fully accomplished the great task of pacifying the Nubians, and the Egyptians regarded him as one of their greatest pharaohs.

Amenemhet III followed Sensuret III with a long and prosperous reign, ordering the construction of an extensive irrigation system in the Fayum desert and turning the region into an agricultural oasis. The subsequent reigns of Amenemhet IV and Queen Sobek Neferu were brief and undistinguished, and little information exists about the breakdown of Egyptian rule that followed. Approximately 70 pharaohs made up the 13th and 14th dynasties, but most were petty princes whose reigns were riddled with strife, and none of them appears to have been able to control Egypt as a whole.

By the 1700s B.C., a people from western Asia had begun to challenge the Egyptians, thus ushering in the Second Intermediate Period (1786-1570 B.C.). The Hyksos, as these newcomers were called, conquered Lower Egypt around 1652 B.C., and they continued to rule the region for the next 150 years. The Egyptian word *hka-hasut*, from which *Hyksos* is derived, meant "Rulers of Foreign Countries."

The Hyksos were a warlike people, and the Egyptians considered them crude and uncivilized. Scholars agree, however, that they brought two very important changes to the Egyptian world. First, they introduced the use of the horse, the chariot, and armor, all of which were to increase the strength of Egyptian armies dramatically. Second, the Hyksos made the Egyptians more aware of the world beyond their native lands. Before the rule of these Asian leaders, most of the Egyptians' expansionist and

commercial interests had been directed toward
Nubia. The reign of the Hyksos would draw the
Egyptians toward deeper involvement with
events in Asia.

Around 1600 B.C., a family from Thebes launched
a series of campaigns against the rulers of the Nile
Delta, and eventually the Hyksos were overwhelmed.
The few texts that have survived from this era docu-
ment the efforts of these 17th-dynasty kings against
their foreign oppressors. According to these sources,
a king named Ahmose drove the foreigners from the
delta and pursued them into Palestine, where he finally broke their power. With Ahmose's victory over
the Hyksos, the age of Egyptian conquest had begun
in earnest.

Ahmose's successful war of liberation made him
the founder of the 18th dynasty. Within a few decades,
his successors conquered a great territory, extending
from the Fourth Cataract of the Nile, in what is now
the Sudan, to the Euphrates River in Syria. The
Egyptian empire grew enormously wealthy from its
expanding commerce and the tribute it demanded
from its vassal states in Africa and Asia. Egypt's imperial age, known as the New Kingdom (1570-1085
B.C.), was an era of unparalleled grandeur.

The first three 18th-dynasty (1570-1314 B.C.)
pharaohs, Amenhotep I, Thutmose I, and Thutmose
II, all carried out campaigns in Nubia and Asia. Thutmose II was followed by Queen Hatshepsut, who ruled
Egypt for 20 peaceful and prosperous years. Hatshepsut sponsored the construction of a number of great
monuments, the most illustrious of which was her
astonishingly beautiful temple at Deir-el-Bahri in
western Thebes. The queen also sent a major expedition to Punt, the successful results of which she had
recorded for posterity on the temple walls.

When Thutmose III finally ascended the throne,

*Tutankhamen, an 18th-dynasty
pharaoh who died while still in
his teens, was buried among
magnificent treasures in the
Valley of the Kings, Thebes.
His inner coffin displayed this
portrait, modeled of gold and
inlaid with precious stones.*

he vented the resentment he had been harboring
against Hatshepsut by destroying the statues that had
been built in her honor and removing her name from
the monuments she had commissioned. Thutmose III
went on to become one of the most remarkable of the
Egyptian pharaohs and one of the greatest military
men in all history. He executed some 17 campaigns in
Africa and Asia and saw his incredible feats recorded
on the walls of Egypt's preeminent national monument, the Temple of Amon at Karnak, near Thebes.

   One of Thutmose's first campaigns was also his
most crucial, for he marched against a coalition

formed by Palestinians, Lebanese, and Syrians in revolt against Egyptian imperialism. After a long and bitter battle, Thutmose vanquished his foes and brought the territory as far north as southern Lebanon under his control. In the 33rd year of his reign, Thutmose III crossed the Euphrates River and defeated the Mitannians on their own soil. He then erected a commemorative stela (a carved stone pillar) next to that of his grandfather, Thutmose I, marking the eastern limit of the Egyptian empire at the Euphrates River. Thutmose later conducted a campaign in Nubia and furthered the colonization of its people. More than any other ruler, Thutmose III was the king who established Egypt as an empire and a world power. Among his most notable monuments are several pairs of magnificent granite obelisks. Today, one of these obelisks, known as Cleopatra's Needle, overlooks London, England, on the bank of the Thames River; its mate can be found in New York City's Central Park.

Thutmose III was succeeded by two able pharaohs, Amenhotep II and Thutmose IV. Amenhotep II spent the years of his reign crushing revolts among the Syrian princes in Asia. Thutmose IV cemented relations with the Asians by marrying a Mittani princess. Queen Mutemwiya, as the foreign bride was called, became the pharaoh's chief consort and the mother of Amenhotep III.

Amenhotep III was pharaoh at a time when Egypt was at the pinnacle of its political, economic, and cultural power. He did not concern himself with military matters, for the ancient world was at peace under Egypt's strong rule. Instead, Amenhotep's reign was distinguished by its remarkable cultural advances. Egypt's royal court, upper class, and emerging middle class all benefited from the unrivaled prosperity of the era, occupying themselves above all with the pursuit of luxury and patronage of the arts.

> Amenhotep III commissioned more monuments than any other 18th-dynasty pharaoh. Only the celebrated Ramses II, a ruler of the 19th dynasty, outstripped him, partly because he reinscribed many of Amenhotep's works and attributed them to himself. Amenhotep's more notable works include his mortuary temple at Thebes, the Temple of Soleb in Nubia, and the Temple of Amon at Luxor. He was succeeded by his son, Amenhotep IV.

After the fifth year of his rule, Amenhotep IV changed his name to Akhenaton in honor of his personal god, Aton. Concerned primarily with spiritual matters, Akhenaton tried to revolutionize Egyptian religion and society, promoting Aton above all other Egyptian gods. Akhenaton moved his palace residence from Thebes to a new capital he called Akhetaton, now known as Tell el-Amarna. He lived out his last 14 years worshiping the creative power of the sun through Aton, the god that had no image.

Akhenaton's revolution died with him. Semenkhka-ra, his successor, quickly abandoned the cult of Aton and reconciled with the traditional priesthood of Amon-Ra. After a three-year reign, he was followed by Tutankhamen (King Tut), who died nine years later at the age of 18. Tutankhamen did not live long enough to prove himself as pharaoh, but the discovery of his tomb in the Valley of the Kings in 1922 remains the most celebrated find in the field of ancient history. Tutankhamen's tomb was small, but, unlike other Egyptian treasures, it remained intact throughout the centuries that followed his death, offering breathtaking evidence of the wealth and art of the 18th dynasty.

Horemheb was the last king of the 18th dynasty. An experienced general, he recognized the weaknesses of the rulers that followed Akhenaton and

seized the throne by force. Horemheb proved an ex-
cellent administrator. He strengthened Egypt's central government and introduced measures to combat
corruption among the officials of his regime.

Horemheb chose an army officer named Pa-
Ramses to succeed him, and with his successor's reign,
the 19th dynasty (1314-1197 B.C.) began. Seti I, Pa-
Ramses' son, was the first of a line of warrior kings who
concentrated on restoring Egypt's international power
and prestige, which had begun to diminish during the
indulgent reign of Amenhotep III. As soon as he
ascended the throne, Seti I defeated the Syrians and
regained control of Palestine. He clashed with Egypt's
main enemy, the Hittites, at the Palestinian city of
Kadesh, but he was unable to break their stronghold
in northern Syria. This task was left to his successor,
Ramses II.

Ramses II prepared to annihilate the Hittites by
moving his entire royal palace and administration to
Per-Ramses, a city in the northeastern Nile Delta,
where he established a military base from which to
launch his Asian campaigns. In 1285 B.C., Ramses and
his army marched to Kadesh to confront a coalition
of more than 20 Asiatic states headed by Mutawallis,
the Hittite king. Ramses' troops, it turned out, were
vastly outnumbered, but they fought so valiantly that
the battle ended in a draw. Ramses had detailed accounts of the Battle of Kadesh and later military
encounters carved on the walls of his monuments at
Karnak in Thebes and Abu Simbel in Nubia. It was
not until the 23rd year of his rule that Ramses II
signed a peace treaty with the Hittite king Hattusilis,
both leaders having found a common foe in the rising
Assyrians. Hattusilis visited Ramses 14 years later,
bringing with him one of his daughters, whom Ramses
took as a bride. The remarkable peace between the
two empires lasted more than 50 years.

Near the end of his reign, Ramses lost his hold on

This relief fragment from a 23rd-dynasty tomb near Thebes depicts an arm holding an ankh, the Egyptian emblem of life.

Egypt's eastern frontier, and Asian armies began to march against him. His son and successor, Merneptah, had to put down revolts in Syria, Palestine, and Libya.

Merneptah's death caused a dynastic struggle as five different rulers, whose identities remain obscure, tried to usurp Egypt's throne. After about 20 years of conflict, a king named Sethnakhr restored order to the empire, thereby beginning the 20th dynasty (1197-1085 B.C.). His son, Ramses III, was the last great pharaoh of the New Kingdom. Ramses III reorganized

the government and the military. He also defended
Egypt against the Libyan tribes, who were attacking
from the northwest, and the so-called Sea Peoples
(dwellers in the Balkans and Black Sea regions), who
had overrun Syria and Palestine and were trying to
invade the Nile Delta. Even during the reign of this
powerful pharaoh, however, signs of political instabil-
ity manifested themselves in labor problems and palace conspiracies.

> After Ramses' death, all manner of political
> and economic chaos ensued: workers struck,
> food prices rose, and Nubia broke away from
> Egyptian rule. Government corruption and dis-
> order increased during the reigns of the pharaohs
> that followed, from Ramses IV to Ramses IX. At
> the same time, the priesthood in Thebes fostered
> superstition among the people, encouraging them
> to believe that Amon-Ra's authority superseded
> that of the pharaoh. So well did they succeed that
> in 1085 B.C. the high priest of Amon-Ra, Heri-
> Hor, was able to usurp the throne and rule Upper
> Egypt. Lower Egypt, meanwhile, fell to the Liby-
> ans. Egypt was once more a land divided.

The era that began with the 21st dynasty is commonly referred to as the Third Intermediate Period
(1085-715 B.C.). The rulers of the 21st dynasty governed Lower Egypt from their capital at Tanis, leaving
Upper Egypt to the descendants of Heri-Hor in
Thebes. Both kingdoms were very weak. The entire
economy of Egypt was rapidly declining, and with it
the pharaohs' military power, which meant the loss of
such territories as Syria and Palestine. As Egypt's
social structure continued to break down, the impov-
erished people began looting the tombs of the phar-

aohs in a desperate effort to support themselves. The priests were forced to take drastic action to save the bodies of the pharaohs from destruction. They ordered workmen to sink a deep shaft into the cliffs at Deir-el-Bahri; within it they placed some 40 mummies from the 18th, 19th, and 20th dynasties, including those of Amenhotep I, Thutmose III, Seti I, Ramses II, and Ramses III. Other mummies, such as that of Amenhotep II, were concealed in tombs that had already been violated. The shaft was discovered in 1881 and Amenhotep II's hiding place in 1898. Since that time, the pharaohs have found a new resting place in the Museum of Antiquities in Cairo.

The 22nd dynasty (950-730 B.C.) was founded by Sheshonq I, a Libyan who helped break the power of the hereditary priests at Thebes. This dynasty remained in power for about 200 years and brought some semblance of stability to the region. Under Sheshonq I, Egypt again became involved in the affairs of neighboring states. Although initially an ally of King Solomon of Jerusalem, Sheshonq eventually plotted against him, and in 935 B.C., during the reign of Solomon's successor, he sent his army out to invade Jerusalem. Egypt was not strong enough to retain its foothold in Palestine, but during the occupation it benefited from an increase in foreign trade.

Around 760 B.C., a Libyan ruler broke away from the 22nd dynasty and set up a rival kingdom in Thebes. This was the beginning of the 23rd dynasty (c.761–c.715 B.C.), an era so chaotic that the order of its few rulers is still disputed. The 24th dynasty (725–710 B.C.) had only one ruler, Tefnakht, who governed with his son, Bahenrenef, at Sais. Around 730 B.C., the Nubians invaded Egypt, ushering in the 25th dynasty under a leader named Piankhi. The 25th dynasty began the Late Period (730-332 B.C.), which continued until the last Egyptian dynasty was destroyed by Alexander the Great in 332 B.C.

The Nubian pharaohs of the 25th dynasty (730-656 B.C.) unified Egypt for almost a century. Theirs was a stable rule, and it brought about a cultural and artistic revival. The Nubian kings bore pharaonic titles, honored the cult of Amon-Ra, restored temples, and preserved ancient texts. Around 664 B.C., the Assyrians invaded Egypt and ended the Nubian era, setting up a new regime in the Nile Delta.

About 10 years into the Assyrians' reign, Psammetichus, an Egyptian prince from Sais, managed with the help of Greek mercenaries to overthrow the Assyrians and reunite Upper and Lower Egypt. The so-called Saite dynasty (654-525 B.C.) marked Egypt's last significant period of native rule. Striving to restore Egypt's power, the Saite kings promoted relations with the Mediterranean countries as well as with Syria and Palestine. They pursued commercial interests abroad, inducing growing numbers of foreign merchants, especially Greeks, to settle in Lower Egypt. The Persian ruler Cambyses ended this revival when he conquered all of Egypt in 525 B.C.

The 27th dynasty effectively finished Egypt as an independent power; under its rule, the country became a province of the Persian empire. Despite this drastic fall from greatness, for centuries Egypt's culture remained largely intact. Egyptian style in the arts changed very little, and the population still used its native tongue and cursive script.

In 404 B.C., a local family overturned the Persians, but the 28th, 29th, and 30th dynasties were only able to maintain their independence for about 60 years. A second Persian dynasty began in 341 B.C.; nine years later Alexander the Great invaded Egypt, drawing its 3,000-year civilization to a close.

2

EGYPTIAN RELIGION

R ELIGION permeated the lives of the ancient
Egyptians, who lived in constant and close
touch with the natural environment. In an effort to
understand the physical world in which they lived,
they deified and personified elements of the natural
world, believing that the presence of the divine was
evident in all nature and had an impact on almost
every aspect of daily life. As they did not view their
lives in terms of spiritual and secular realms, as does
modern man, they had no word for the concept of
religion.

The Egyptian gods were remarkably varied in char-
acter and form. In prehistoric times, every town had
its own local deity or family of gods, and each was
worshiped in its own temple. The people believed that
if they properly cared for and attended to the gods,
they would receive such benefits as prosperity, protection, long life, and an orderly society.

Political solidarity united many of these independent cults, and some deities were assimilated into

*A rabbit and a serpent confront each other next to a portrait of
Apep, a sun god, in a tomb painting from Deir-el-Medina.
Animals played an important role in Egyptian religion, figuring
prominently in stories of magic and intermingling with the world
of the gods.*

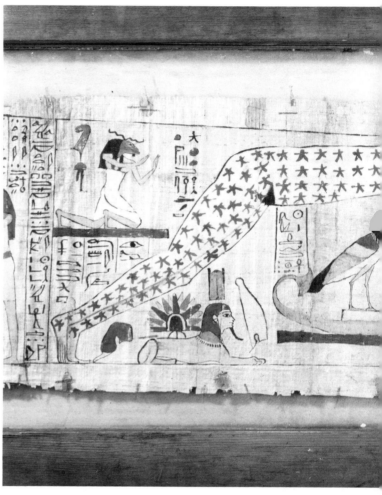

Nut, goddess of the sky, spans the space above Shu, god of the air (center right, both arms raised), and Geb, god of the earth (reclining), in an illustration of the Egyptian creation myth.

others. Thus, some of the gods had both animal and human features and characteristics. The Egyptians even made a place in their pantheon for foreign gods. Moreover, whenever a certain town gained prominence, its gods assumed greater power and prestige. At the same time, however, the nation's central authority encouraged the growth of an official pantheon of gods, with one supreme god at the top.

The Egyptians explained the history of the universe through myths, or stories about the gods. The oldest gods were associated with the creation of the world. Several Egyptian stories deal with the first

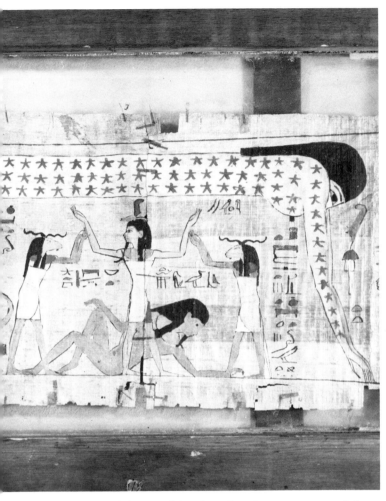

morning of the world, when land was separated from water, lightness from darkness, and the earth from the sky. The most ancient creation story originated in the town of Heliopolis, whose local god, Atum, is the oldest of the principal deities. According to this myth, a mound of earth appeared out of *Nun*, the primordial waters. From this earth emerged Atum, who took a human form. Because the power of the setting sun was associated with Atum, his appearance from the depths of the primordial waters symbolized light coming out of the darkness.

After his emergence, Atum made, from his body,

the first pair of gods: Shu, the god of air, and Tefnut, the goddess of moisture. This couple gave birth to Geb and Nut, the god of earth and the goddess of sky, respectively. Geb and Nut clung together until Shu placed Nut high up in the sky, then filled the distance between the sky and earth with his breath, the air.

Geb and Nut gave birth to Osiris, Isis, Seth, and Nephtys. These children of the gods became earth's first inhabitants and ruled the world. The story involving the relationship among Osiris, Seth, and Isis is probably the most fascinating of all Egyptian myths. Osiris was the first king of Egypt. Good as well as wise, he civilized Egypt and taught humans many things. While he reigned, the world was prosperous and just. But Seth became jealous of his brother and devised a scheme to get rid of him. He made a beautiful chest and offered it to Osiris as a gift. Pleased, Osiris got into the chest to see if he could fit inside. Seth then slammed the lid shut and heaved the chest into the Nile. Osiris drowned.

Isis, Osiris's bereaved sister-wife, relentlessly searched for the chest containing her husband's body. She finally found it concealed in a tree in Syria, brought it back to Egypt, and hid it from Seth. One day, while Seth was out hunting, he happened to find the chest. Flying into a fit of jealous rage, he hacked Osiris's body into 14 pieces and flung them to the farthest regions of Egypt. But faithful Isis did not give up. She sadly gathered each and every piece, put Osiris's body back together, and, using her magical powers, brought him back to life. Before Osiris had to return to the world of the dead, of which he was king, he and Isis conceived a child, a boy who would be named Horus.

Raising Horus secretly in the Delta, Isis trained him to have only one goal in life: to avenge his father's death and reclaim the throne of Egypt. The day of reckoning produced a long and bloody battle. Seth, at

This bronze statue from the 26th dynasty shows the Egyptian goddess Isis in a characteristic pose, seated and nursing her son, Horus.

one point, gouged out Horus's eye, but Thoth, the god of wisdom, healed the eye and restored it to Horus. Horus, the rightful heir, finally prevailed, and a tribunal of gods placed him on the throne of Egypt.

To the Egyptians, the Osiris myth symbolized certain forces of the natural world, showing how universal order depended on a constant balancing act between those forces. Wicked and unjust, Seth created chaos and disorder in the world. He represented the desert—a barren, burning, almost totally uninhabitable place—and was associated with such animals as the crocodile, the hippopotamus, and the aardvark. Horus's battle with Seth was seen as a warring between the forces of light and darkness, or good and evil.

Horus represented all that was good in a just ruler. As the obedient son, he avenged his father's death, then carried out the necessary burial rites, thereby presenting an example for all Egyptians to follow. Horus was also identified with the noonday, or youthful, sun. This aspect of his power was manifested in the falcon, a bird that the Egyptians believed capable of flying close to the sun. Horus, therefore, commonly took the form of a vigorous young male with a falcon's head topped by a sun disk.

Egyptians took the story of Osiris to heart. His death and rebirth explained the cycle of life; he stood for fertility and the new crops that flourished every year after the Nile had overflowed its banks. Osiris represented every green plant that entered and nourished the body of all living things. His resurrection seemed to mean that others, too, could be born again. Because the Egyptians clung to a belief in an afterlife, they developed an elaborate method of preserving the

bodies of their dead. According to tradition, the first body to be made into a mummy was that of Osiris.

Completing the divine family image, Isis represented the perfect wife and mother. Egyptians cherished the story of her search for Osiris's remains, her powerful incantations to restore him, and her delivery of Horus, whom she raised in secret and guarded from his evil uncle. Isis is most often depicted as the seated mother, holding or nursing her son. She is also shown standing with upraised wings, symbolic of her protective powers. The great love, loyalty, and devotion Isis expressed for her family set a pattern for other women to follow. She was honored as the source of women's wisdom and mysterious powers, which far exceeded those of mortal men or even of other gods. She also safeguarded all Egyptian traditions, customs, and myths.

Among the other gods created at the world's beginning were Ma'at and her associate, Thoth. Ma'at represented truth and moral order in the universe, the maintaining of which required constant vigilance by both gods and humans. The goddess was usually pictured wearing an ostrich feather on her head, symbolizing truth and justice.

Thoth, who was connected with wisdom, the intellect, and magic, was the messenger and secretary of the gods. Greatly respected for his keen intellect, he was called the "master of the word" by the Egyptians. Thoth invented hieroglyphs, the picture-writing system of the Egyptians, and was, therefore, the god of scribes. Because he was associated with the moon, Thoth was also the keeper of time. He ruled the seasons and determined when people would be born and when they would die. Thoth was often pictured as an ibis—perhaps because the bird's crescent-shaped beak resembled a half-moon—but he also took the form of a baboon. Portraits of scribes of the time frequently show them with a baboon, the symbol of inspiration and learning, on their shoulders.

The pharaoh occupied an important position in the Egyptians' religious worldview. His father was the country's main god, and his mother, the previous pharaoh's principal queen. So he was both divine and human, and likened to Horus, whose birthright had

A 28th-dynasty tomb painting depicts women mourning the loss of a loved one. Veneration of the dead was an important part of Egyptian religious practice.

been the throne of Egypt. The pharaoh was seen as an intermediary between the gods and humankind.

The pharaoh's primary obligation, both to the gods and to humanity, was to maintain harmony in the world. He pledged to protect the land and its people from all enemies. Each day he per-

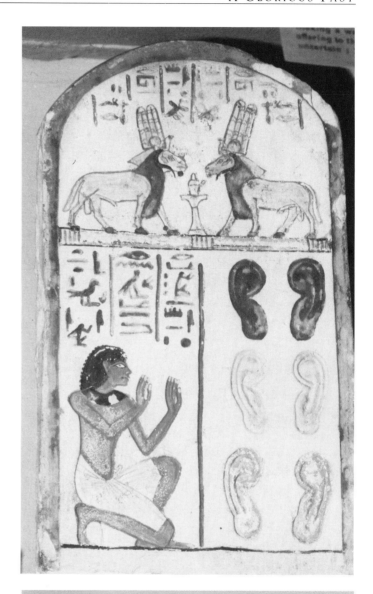

This votive stela has been decorated with three sets of ears to ensure that worshipers' prayers will be heard.

formed sacred rituals to ensure that the Nile would flood the land every year, the earth would remain fertile, and the sun rise and set every day. In this manner, the survival of humankind was assured. The Egyptian people repaid the pharaoh for his care by promising him service, self-sacrifice, and loyalty. When the pharaoh died, he

was, like Osiris, born again; the heir to his throne
became the new Horus. Once more, Egypt was
saved from primeval chaos, and universal harmony was maintained.

The Egyptian pantheon contained two other preeminent gods: Ptah, originally sacred to the city of
Memphis, and Amon-Ra, patron of the city of
Thebes. The Memphite priests developed a very sophisticated doctrine to explain the creation of the
universe. According to their account, the Memphite
Theology, Ptah created the world by first conceiving
of it intellectually (the center of the intellect was the
heart) and then "thinking" the gods, human beings,
animals, and all other earthly things into being. Ptah,
as was true of most Egyptian deities, had multiple roles
and titles. Like Ma'at, he was associated with truth
and the world's moral order. As the creator god, Ptah
was also the patron of artists and craftsmen, including
painters, metalworkers, and sculptors.

Amon was originally a little-known god from
Thebes. During the reign of the twelfth-dynasty kings,
Amon became the chief Theban god after the Hyksos
were expelled in his name. Word of Amon's power
and prestige spread throughout the Egyptian empire.
During the New Kingdom, he took on the attributes
of the sun god, Ra, of Heliopolis, and was called
Amon-Ra. Amon's power continued to grow: the
Egyptians regarded him as king of all the gods, even
claiming that he chose the pharaohs by making his
wishes known through an oracle. Amon-Ra was sometimes pictured as a man wearing a sun disk, or sometimes as a ram with large curved horns, indicative of
his fertility and virility.

Ordinary people could not enter the inner
sanctuaries of the great national temples to worship; instead, priests acting on their behalf per-

formed the daily rituals for the state gods. Nevertheless, religion was extremely important in everyday life. The average citizen participated in the national religious festivals and ceremonies, worshiped his or her personal gods, and believed in and practiced magic.

The great religious festivals gave the masses an opportunity to experience their faith publicly and on a grand scale. There were several festivals each month; some celebrated agricultural events, others were associated with the gods, still others with the pharaohs. Thebes, for example, was the center of two major festivals dedicated to Amon.

The festival of Opet took place at the beginning of the year, coinciding with the start of the floods. The priests took the statue of Amon—as well as those of his consort, the goddess Mut, and his son, the god Khonsu—from the sanctuary at the Temple of Karnak and placed all three in sacred boats. The statue-carrying vessels were propelled about a mile and a half up the Nile, then placed on the priests' shoulders and carried to the Temple of Luxor in a procession. The festival was a great spectacle, accompanied by carnival-like gaiety. People crowded along the route, entertainers sang and danced, peddlers hawked their goods, and people threw flowers, drank beer, and ate their fill of rich meats, breads, and pastries.

The priests stopped the procession six times along the route to allow the people to ask questions of Amon. They manipulated the god's statue to nod yes or no in answer to direct questions. In the evening, the boats carried the statues back to Karnak, and the festivities were repeated the following day. By the end of the New Kingdom era, the Opet festival lasted as long as 27 days.

During the 10th month of the year, Amon was taken across the Nile to visit the west bank. Here were the desert cliffs where the dead were buried: rulers in the Valley of the Kings, nobility in their elaborate tombs, members of the middle class in the fanciest tombs they could afford, and poor people, who were buried in shallow graves on the outskirts of the desert.

This special festival enabled the Egyptians to honor and, they believed, communicate with the spirits of the dead. Entertainment, feasting, and drinking lasted all night long. Reverence for ancestors persisted throughout Egypt. Each individual cared for the graves of family members, just as the priests cared for the mortuary temples of the gods on behalf of all Egyptians. The people carried images of the dead in the national procession, then went to their family grave sites for private feasts. In niches in their homes, the Egyptians also kept statues representing the souls of their deceased relatives.

Because most people had limited contact with the state gods, they turned to more personal gods for protection and assistance in their daily lives. They worshiped these gods in shrines in their homes or outdoors in natural settings. People in small communities, probably unable to support a priesthood, organized religious activities themselves. For instance, at the village of Deir-el-Medina, home of the craftsmen who built the royal tombs during the New Kingdom, residents erected public shrines, statuettes, and stelae, to which people made offerings and prayed. Stelae representing gods often had carved ears to enable them to hear worshipers' prayers.

Bes and Tawaret were two of the most popular gods associated with the house and family. Bes, a dwarf with a lion's face and an ugly grin, wielded a sword and shield. His frightening appearance was supposed to protect the home from evil spirits. Bes was also the carrier of joy to the home, and so was frequently portrayed dancing and playing music.

Tawaret, who resembled a hippopotamus, was the

goddess of childbearing. The Egyptians had observed that these great creatures seemed to give birth easily and with little pain. Tawaret was, naturally, of special importance to women, who prayed to her for safe delivery of their children. Because female hippopotamuses were seen to guard their young with great ferocity, Tawaret was also regarded as a protector of the home.

Like most ancient peoples, the Egyptians believed in the power of magic. To them, the entire universe was alive with spirits, some of them kindly toward humans, but many malicious and harmful. No one worried much about the good ones, but the evil spirits had to be placated with the art of magic, which was considered a gift from the gods to help man control the supernatural. Bad magic was performed to harm people, and good magic was believed to be beneficial. It was the priests who carefully studied the art and learned the rites, incantations, and charms necessary to cast spells.

Amulets, small objects worn on the body, were the most common form of protective magic available. They were made of a variety of materials: papyrus, wood, leather, or stone. On them were written the names of gods, nonsense words, magical prayers, diagrams, and powerful symbols representing such concepts as strength, prosperity, and life. Figures of Bes and Tawaret were worn as amulets, as was the popular *udjat-eye*. This was the eye of Horus, knocked out by Seth during their battle and restored by Thoth. It protected against the evil eye and symbolized light. The scarab beetle and the ankh (sign of life) were other common amulets that protected their wearers from evil forces.

The Egyptians also used wands made from hippopotamus bone, which they placed near their beds at night to protect them from dangerous animals, poisonous scorpions, and snakes. The wands were considered powerful because of the strength of the hippo. In addition, to determine which days were best and which were unsafe for certain activities, people used calendars. Dreams were taken very seriously, and texts were written to interpret their significance. Like other ancient peoples, the Egyptians created a rich and diverse system for explaining how the universe came into being, how it was maintained, and what role human beings played within it.

3

LIFE IN THE NILE VALLEY

THE foundation of Egyptian society was the family. Men and women were encouraged to marry and to establish households at an early age. A saying of the time was "If thou art a man of note, found for thyself a household and love thy wife. Feed her, clothe her, and give her ointment for her limbs. Gladden her heart so long as she liveth."

The Egyptians generally married within the same social class, and sometimes within the same family. Scholars once thought that Egyptians permitted marriage between brothers and sisters, because in Egyptian texts the terms for brother and sister often appear in place of the words for husband and wife. It is now known that these were common terms of endearment and that it was highly unusual—despite the Isis and Osiris myth—for an Egyptian to marry a family member more closely related than a cousin.

Egyptian women possessed legal rights that were exceptional for the time. They could buy, own, and sell property. They could divorce, and when they did so they could make claims on certain family possessions. Still, the status of women was by no means equal to that of men. A woman's primary task was to care

This wall painting from a tomb at Luxor, near Thebes, shows Egyptian craftsmen casting bronze, a metal introduced to Egypt from Asia during the Middle Kingdom.

51

for her husband, children, and home. Her daily life was filled with such ordinary domestic tasks as brewing beer, baking bread, spinning, and weaving. Egyptian women were seldom taught to read or write, skills that would have been required in order to enter into any of the professions. Normally, the only occupations open to women were those of musician, priestess, dancer, and, more rarely, shopkeeper.

To Egyptians, a marriage was incomplete without children. The birth of a boy was looked upon as a special blessing, because boys grew up to become the providers and protectors of the family, but girls were loved as well. Children often followed their parents about as they did their daily work in the home, fields, or shops, and in this way they learned the family trade or craft. Among commoners, a more formal education was reserved for those privileged boys who trained for the position of scribe, a notable profession that often led to more lucrative jobs and higher social status. Girls seldom received formal schooling; they were expected to stay in the home, and their mothers showed them how to perform their domestic duties. Egyptian parents taught their children to be honest, humble, well behaved, and respectful of their elders. Children are easily recognized in Egyptian art; they are usually naked, they wear their hair in a side knot, with the rest of their head clean-shaven, and they are often pictured covering their mouths with their fingers.

Egyptian households often included a family pet. Dogs and cats held a special place in the Egyptian family; tomb paintings of Egyptian men and women performing everyday activities often include images of these animals.

The Egyptians lived in town houses and villas. Those who resided in the empire's crowded villages or cities stayed in a town house. These buildings, which ranged in size from one to three stories, were arranged in tightly packed rows, and each had a front door that opened directly onto the narrow street. The women who lived in these houses frequently carried out their household duties on the roof. Sometimes the family also slept on the roof, where the night air was cooler. The windows of town houses were placed high up, to give the family privacy, allow heat to escape, and keep out the sun's glare.

The wealthy, who could afford larger plots of land, lived outside the city. Their ideal home was the one-storied, spacious country villa, surrounded by courtyards, landscaped gardens, and scenic pools with waterfowl, fish, and lotus blossoms. These houses had separate quarters for living, entertaining, and working. The family's private rooms, baths, and entertaining areas were usually located in the center of the estate. The workshops, stables, and servants' quarters were situated in outbuildings encircling the mansion. Egyptian villas were protected by a high, mud-brick wall that was whitewashed to reflect the heat of the sun.

The rich possessed beautiful utilitarian objects and could afford to decorate their homes handsomely. They enhanced their walls and floors with murals painted in bright colors. Their furnishings included elegant, expertly crafted beds, chairs, and chests. Ordinary people made do with a few wooden tables and chairs.

Egypt's climate called for loose clothing made of lightweight fabrics in pale colors; the Egyptians favored white linen. Upper-class men wore clean, white skirts, or kilts, which came in as many as 40 different styles: short or long, plain or pleated. The basic garment for women was a simple, sleeveless dress. Egyptian art always shows this garment fitting closely to a woman's body, but the Egyptian dresses that have

Magic eyes gaze out from a wooden house facade, one example of the rich ornamentation in the homes of Egypt's wealthy.

survived from the period are actually loose and free-flowing. The dresses were held up by shoulder straps and sometimes tied with a sash underneath the bodice.

Fashions changed over time, although the kilt and the dress remained the basic costumes for men and women throughout the history of ancient Egypt. In the Middle Kingdom, the men added a tunic—a shirtlike garment for the upper body—as well as a cloak, often worn over one shoulder. Men also took to wearing a longer version of the kilt, a garment somewhat like a toga that was fastened up over the chest and fell below the knees. This garment was often pleated and fringed. During the New Kingdom, Egyptian fashion became very elaborate, especially in women's clothing. Wealthy women turned the basic dress into an undergarment, sheathing it in a beautifully pleated, fringed, and billowy robe. Some Egyptians wore sandals made of woven rushes or leather, but many chose to go barefoot.

Egyptian peasants wore simple clothing that allowed them to move freely as they worked. The men might simply tie a rough cloth around their hips; the women made do with the basic dress. The Egyptians were not self-conscious about their bodies, and in many instances they were content to go partially clothed or naked. Tomb paintings show that men frequently tied their loincloths around their waist or did away with them altogether when working hard under the hot sun. Likewise, tomb sculptures and paintings of women grinding grain and brewing beer show that they tied their dresses down around their hips when working.

The Egyptians' pristine, white clothing served as the setting for brilliantly colored jewelry. They rarely wore patterned or colored cloth; in Egyptian paintings, the people who are shown wearing colors and patterns are generally foreigners and servants. The costume of the wealthy Egyptian was not complete without necklaces, earrings, arm and ankle bracelets, and rings. The collar necklace, or *usekh*, which meant "the broad one," was one of the most popular forms of adornment. Made of many strands of beads, it was designed to lie splendidly upon the shoulders of the wearer.

The Egyptians, like most other people, liked to be seen at their best. Each morning began with a bath of water and soda: the wealthy bathed and changed into fresh clothes more than once a day. The drying effects of the sun and dust required Egyptian men and women to keep their skin moisturized with oils. Oil of lily was one of the fancier perfumed concoctions available. Egyptian art contains charming scenes showing wealthy women attending to their toilet while pretty young servant girls help them with their wigs or braid their hair in styles similar to those worn by women today. To mask unpleasant odors, women often wore garlands of flowers in their hair or small, scented cosmetic cones on top of their head. The cones were made from animal fat blended with fragrant oil; tomb paintings of banquet scenes suggest that the cones were allowed to melt over the hair and upper body for their moisturizing benefits and pleasing aroma. Artists represented this process by coloring the shoulders and chest areas of the Egyptians' white garments yellow and orange.

Dating as far back as 4000 B.C., Egyptian men and women outlined their eyes with kohl, a black pigment that enhanced their appearance and protected them from the sun's glare. They made rouge and lipstick from red ocher (earth) mixed with fat, and red nail polish from the juice of the henna plant. Men usually kept their faces clean-shaven except for a small mustache or goatee; hairiness was considered unclean and barbaric. The upper classes often shaved their heads or kept their hair short, and adorned themselves with wigs and hairpieces. Wigs could be short or long—straight, curly, or braided.

Most Egyptians were farmers, and they led a harsh life, working from sunrise to sunset. Tomb paintings illustrate in tireless detail the steps a farmer had to go through to cultivate wheat and barley, Egypt's primary crops. When it was time to harvest, the pharaoh's official overseer, known by historians as the field scribe, would come out to account for the crop. He would survey the grain fields with a measuring line in order to decide how much the farmer should pay in taxes. The farmer had little choice in the matter. If he refused to pay, he was simply given a sound thrashing. Ultimately, a large part of the harvest that farmers produced went to pay taxes. Farmers also had to pay rent on their land, for it did not belong to them. Normally, the fields a farmer worked were attached to the estates of the pharaoh, a wealthy landowner, or the priests belonging to a rich temple complex.

From June to September, when the Nile Valley was flooded, many farmers were drafted into the services of the pharaoh. They usually took part in various building projects, joining the regular force of craftsmen employed to work on the monuments. This unpaid labor service, or corve duty, was required of all Egyptians except officials. Those who could afford to do so paid to be exempted from service. The poor, therefore, were overburdened when "duty" called. Their labor was exploited for the construction of public buildings, the building and maintenance of Egypt's extensive irrigation systems, and the cultivation of the pharaoh's land. If a peasant tried to escape corve duty, the law considered him a fugitive, and if he was caught, he was subject to imprisonment. He and his family could also be forced into permanent servitude to the state. It is a common misconception that the Egyptians forced great numbers of foreign slaves to build such magnificent monuments as the Great Pyramids of Giza. There were slaves in Egyptian society, but they were few in number, and the country's mighty monuments were built by the common laborer.

Agriculture, the basis of the Egyptian economy, became the theme of extensive tomb paintings. In this 18th-dynasty scene, a pair of field laborers transport grain while two girls fight in the background.

The plight of the peasant improved under the reforms passed by the Middle Kingdom pharaohs. Those who worked the land were still tied to large estates, but each farmer was assigned his own lot,

which meant he had more control over his own affairs.

Besides the majority of Egyptians, who were peasants, and the small minority that made up the ruling class, there was a sizable group of craftsmen, soldiers, scribes, lesser officials, and priests who might be said to make up a middle class. Recent archaeological excavations have shed more light on the life of the craftsman, one of the most vital members of this class.

Many Egyptians were involved in the craft industries, and most, like the farmers, worked for the pharaoh, the state, or the priests. Such craftsmen were organized into workshops or communities under an overseer. They were not seen as artists, but as skilled workmen who produced objects and images of beauty, high technical achievement, and practicality. Craftspeople provided Egyptians with the basic items necessary for everyday life. Egyptian craft industries included glass-making, painting, sculpture, weaving, metallurgy, jewelry-making, carpentry, shipbuilding, cabinetmaking, the production of papyrus, and masonry. Pictorial representations have left a wealth of information about the materials, techniques, and tools used by Egyptian craftsmen. Excavations at Deir-el-Medina, a village community of workers established during the New Kingdom, have given historians an even clearer picture of what daily life was like for the artisan class.

Deir-el-Medina was set up early in the 18th dynasty and survived for more than 400 years. This highly specialized community operated exclusively as a workshop for the construction of tombs. It was located at the foot of the desert cliffs in southwestern Thebes. Most of the work was carried out in secret, and the workers possessed all the skills necessary to construct the magnificent tombs that can still be seen in the Valley of the Kings. Their tasks included the cutting and transporting of stone from desert quarries, the mixing of mortar, and the construction and decoration of the tomb's walls. The main workers, then, were stonemasons, plasterers, sculptors, painters, draftsmen, and carpenters.

The population at Deir-el-Medina was about 300,

which amounted to some 80 families. The workers were divided into two gangs, each of which was led by a foreman, whose position (like that of most craft occupations) was hereditary. Two official scribes worked closely with the foremen, governing the workers and the entire village, keeping track of the tools and other supplies, recording absences, and accounting for and distributing wages. Female slaves were assigned to the village to take care of domestic chores.

The craftsmen were on the job 8 out of 10 days for about six months of the year. They were paid with such goods as barley and wheat (from which they made bread and beer), fish, vegetables, and oils. When they were not at work at Deir-el-Medina, many of them had the option of working for the nobility in Thebes. These craftsmen, then, were fairly affluent, as suggested by the fine tombs they constructed for their own burial. The standard of living at Deir-el-Medina was probably higher than that of most craftspeople. The craftsmen took pride in their work, calling themselves "servants in the Place of Truth," and developed a strong identity as highly skilled and well-regarded artisans. During the uncertain times of the late New Kingdom, when wage distribution became irregular, the craftsmen of Deir-el-Medina even went on strike, enacting one of the earliest labor demonstrations in recorded history.

Another important member of Egypt's middle class was the scribe. Scribes kept the pharaoh's government running smoothly by keeping accounts of the state's affairs. There were scribes to take care of the taxes, the treasury, and the army; many were employed at the palace, and many others worked at temple complexes. The priests who governed the temples owned vast lands, kept huge herds of livestock, and employed thousands of people, and they needed numerous scribes to account for all their transactions. Scribes trained as tax collectors surveyed the land,

Field scribes measure and record grain production for tax purposes. Just as American citizens pay income tax, Egyptian farmers had to pay the pharaoh in proportion to the yield of their acreage.

took the census (counting people and animals), and kept track of the workers' production. Army scribes were needed to enlist military personnel, to distribute and maintain supplies, and to carry messages on the battlefield. The scribe was everywhere with his palette and pen. His job was laborious, complex, and highly respected.

Amenhotep-son-of-Hapu was one of the most

celebrated among Egyptian scribes. He started his career by keeping records of army recruitment, then became chief architect, and finally achieved the second-highest post in the land, that of vizier (a sort of prime minister) to the pharaoh. After his death, he was revered as one of Egypt's greatest wise men and worshiped as a god. His sayings were still popular more than a thousand years after his death.

This 18th-dynasty scene represents Nakht, a scribe and priest under Thutmose IV, hunting with his family along the Nile.

While employed as an architect and engineer, Amenhotep specialized in the construction and transportation of colossal monuments. Two of his most impressive works remain the colossal statues of the pharaoh Amenhotep III. These enormous sculptures once graced the entrance to a vast temple complex that he had also created. During a great earthquake in A.D. 27, the statues were severely cracked, and for years afterward, they emitted twanging sounds that resembled the plucking of harp strings. The people of Egypt maintained that the statues were singing in honor of the sun god Ra as he rose in the eastern sky each morning. Actually, the sounds came from the expanding and contracting of the cracks or spaces in the stone, as the moisture that had gathered during the night dried in the heat of the sun. People began coming from distant lands to hear the statues sing. The Colossi of Memnon, as they came to be known, were for many years one of the ancient world's most popular tourist attractions. Around A.D. 200, the Roman emperor Septimus Severus repaired the statues, thereby ending their song to the sun god.

The Egyptians who could afford to indulged in a large variety of pastimes. Almost everyone played senet, a board game similar to backgammon. Another favorite board game was known as hounds and jackals.

Upper-class Egyptian families enjoyed fishing and hunting fowl among the tall papyrus reeds that grew along the banks of the Nile. Tomb paintings indicate that a man would usually lead the fishing or hunting party; his wife might assist him by helping him keep his balance as he speared fish or threw a boomerang to stun his prey. Children helped carry the catch or entertained themselves by picking water lilies or lotus blossoms. Apparently, even the house servants accompanied the family on such outings, and the family cat helped flush out birds that were hiding in the reeds.

The nobility were especially fond of big-game hunting. They would set out over the desert in light, horse-drawn chariots in pursuit of antelope, gazelle, ostrich, or desert hare. Hunting dogs helped to bring the game down, and the hunter would follow with a bow and arrow or javelin. Young nobles also enjoyed bull baiting and lion hunting—the lion being a native of the Nile Valley in ancient times.

The Egyptians' favorite form of amusement, however, was probably eating, drinking, and socializing. The many banquet scenes that appear in tomb paintings indicate that the Egyptians liked to be well fed and well entertained. Guests would arrive at a party in their best white linen garments, set off with elaborate wigs, collar necklaces, and other finery. They consumed huge quantities of meat, fowl, breads, pastries, and fruit, and washed them all down with copious amounts of beer and wine. Egyptian dinner parties were disorderly, loud, and lively affairs, with guests eating and drinking to excess, often making themselves sick in the process.

To entertain his guests, a host provided dancers and musicians. The dancers were usually servant or slave girls who had been specially trained for such purposes. They might give slow, sensuous performances or engage in wild acrobatics, executing cartwheels, somersaults, back bends, and splits. Music was

Musicians and dancers entertain guests at an Egyptian banquet. From the 18th dynasty on, music was one of the few Egyptian professions in which women prevailed.

essential at such events. Harps of all sizes were the preferred instruments; they accompanied singers of ballads and religious hymns. One of the most popular songs of the time, called "Song of the Harper," aptly conveys the Egyptian philosophy of life:

> Rejoice and let your heart forget that day when
> you shall be laid to rest
> Cast all sorrow behind you and think of
> joy until there comes that day of reaching port
> in the land that loveth silence
> Follow your desire as long as you live, put myrrh
> on your head, clothe yourself in fine linen
> Put singing and music before your face
> Increase even more the delights which you have
> and do not let your heart grow faint
> Follow your inclination and your profit
> Do your desires upon earth, and trouble not your heart
> until that day of lamentation comes to you
> Spend a happy day and be not weary
> For none may take his goods with him, and none
> that hath gone may come again.

4

"LAND OF THE BURNT FACES"

To the ancient Greeks and Romans, Nubia was one of the world's great civilizations. They called it *Aethiopia*—"Land of the Burnt Faces," in Greek—a reference to the dark skin of the region's inhabitants. Herodotus, the Greek historian, proclaimed the Nubians to be the "tallest and most handsome of men." He believed that they ate only milk and boiled meat, and that as a result they lived to the age of 120. The Romans thought the Nubians were ruled only by queens, that they could carve a whole temple from a single stone, and that they lived in translucent houses.

Although these accounts were, of course, only fables, there is no mistaking Nubia's preeminence as an African civilization of enormous power, wealth, and influence. Nubia stretched for 1,000 miles along the Nile River, reaching from modern-day Aswan in southern Egypt to Khartoum in northern Sudan. The Nubian empire flourished for 5,000 years, outlasting the classical civilizations of Greece and Rome as well

In this tomb painting from Thebes, dramatically clothed Nubian women take part in a public procession.

69

as that of Egypt, Nubia's major ally and rival to the north. The Nubians conquered Egypt in the late 8th century and ruled it for nearly 100 years.

Archaeologists (scientists who study the remains of ancient cultures) believe that the first Nubian culture emerged in northern Nubia about 3800 B.C. The people were ruled by a line of kings, possibly predating by several generations the appearance of Egypt's ancient rulers, the pharaohs. Some scholars, in fact, label Nubia's monarchy the earliest in human history.

The early Nubians buried their dead, along with cosmetics and pottery, in stone-lined pits. These people produced "eggshell" pottery, a distinctive type of thin, delicate earthenware decorated with geometric patterns and crosshatch designs in red, ocher, and cream.

History's first reference to the Nubians appears in Egyptian written records, which mention not only military expeditions against the Nubians but trading expeditions as well—for ebony, cattle, slaves, ivory, and stone. The Egyptians called the region *Ta-Seti*, or "land of the bow," a reference to its famed archers. The fourth-dynasty pharaoh Snefru) achieved a momentous victory over the Nubians around 2600 B.C. According to Snefru's historians, the Egyptians carried off 7,000 people and 200,000 head of cattle as war booty. The northern conquerors ruled Nubia for the next three centuries, building forts and establishing towns along the Nile River. Nubia was exploited for its rich deposits of diorite, a type of volcanic rock favored by the Egyptians for building their royal pyramids. They also continued to trade with the Nubians for such exotic and luxurious goods as incense, perfumes, and oils.

The Egyptians usually described their enemies as "wretched and vile," and the Nubians were no exception. Egyptian pharaohs often had representations of the Nubians carved on the bottom of their sandals, so that they were always trampling upon their enemy.

The 12th-dynasty pharaohs sought even more control over the Nubians. Amenemhet I, who is believed to have been part Nubian, initiated this effort by building a series of forts along the Nile River on a 50-mile stretch called the "Belly of the Rocks" because of its dangerous rapids. These colossal forts, all within signaling distance of one another, were supposed to protect the caravan and river traffic from the desert tribes, keep the Nubians from trading in the north, and secure the southern borders. Egypt, though, plagued by internal troubles, was forced to abandon its forts and withdraw from Nubia about 1700 B.C. Nubia was left alone to continue developing on its own.

By 2000 B.C., a city-state archaeologists call Kerma had emerged in Nubia. Taking advantage of its trade with Egypt and exposure to the country's technology and culture, Kerma soon became a nation of great sophistication and wealth. Gold, which was discovered in the Nubian deserts at this time, became one of the most important commodities in Kerma-Egypt trade. After the Kerma kings gained control of the Upper Nile, they built small forts to protect their trade routes and began demanding higher prices from the Egyptians for their goods. Egyptians involved in the export trade lived in permanent settlements in Kerma. It was during this period that the Egyptians started to call Ta-Seti *Kush.*

The powerful kings of Kerma cultivated an expensive taste for luxuries. To prepare for their own burials, they constructed huge circular mounds called *tumuli.* A dead king was laid out on a gold-ornamented funer-

A Nubian slave carrying a jar provides the form for this Egyptian makeup box from around 1350 B.C.

ary bed placed in the most magnificent of the tomb's many chambers. Each of these rooms, whose walls were painted in brilliant colors, was filled with beautiful gold, ivory, and bronze objects. And in the central corridor, as many as 400 servants, dressed in their finest garments, were buried alive with their king.

The arts flowered under this stable government. Kerma culture was influenced by Egyptian art forms, technology, and concepts, but the state's artists elaborated on the basic Egyptian models with their own native designs to create objects unique to Kerma. Especially skilled in pottery and metalwork, Kerma's craftsmen made jewelry with carnelian and gold beads, and faience, an exquisite type of earthenware decorated with colored glazes. Artists used mica to make decorative inlays shaped like animals, mythical creatures, and plants. Potters produced a great variety of objects in many sizes, shapes, colors, and with extensive designs.

The most beautiful and original of this pottery is called Kerma blacktopped ware. These delicate, elegantly designed pieces have smooth, polished surfaces. The upper portion is black, the lower, dark red, and around the center runs a cream-colored strip. This fine pottery was apparently widely produced as well as highly valued; hundreds of examples have been discovered in Kerma burial sites.

Egypt's New Kingdom era (1570-1085 B.C.) marked the end of Kerma's autonomy. Initiating a campaign to colonize Nubia, Pharaoh Ahmose I installed a viceroy (governor), called the "King's son of Kush," to rule Nubia. Ahmose's successors continued the colonization effort, which was strongly resisted by the Nubians. The pharaohs also began the practice of taking Nubian princes back to their royal courts; brought up as Egyptians, the princes were expected to support Egypt when they were sent back to their home country. By the 19th dynasty (1314-1197 B.C.), Nubia was under Egypt's firm control.

The Nubians rapidly adopted Egyptian customs. They buried their royalty in small pyramids decorated with stelae, hieroglyphic inscriptions, and tomb paintings. Many Nubians worked in the gold mines and were involved in various commercial activities. Other Nubians had jobs as soldiers or police. Occupations at a higher level, such as those of merchant, military officer, or priest, were usually given to Egyptians. In addition, Egyptians who settled in Nubia usually lived on the banks of the Nile and formed their own compounds, which became strong centers of Egyptian culture.

As symbols of their power in Nubia, the New Kingdom pharaohs built magnificent temples in the country. Amenhotep III erected one of the finest monuments, built in Soleb and dedicated to the god Amon-Ra. He also erected a temple in Sedeinga for his wife, Queen Tiye, a commoner from southern Egypt who may have been Nubian. Ramses II, the greatest builder of all the pharaohs, also left his mark on Nubia. The most celebrated of his numerous monuments there remains the Great Temple of Ramses II at Abu Simbel. This rock-hewn structure, actually cut out of the sandstone cliffs, was dedicated to the gods Amon-Ra, Re-Harakhty, Ptah, and Hathor, but it also deified Ramses himself, as well as his favorite royal wife, Queen Nofretari.

After holding sway over Nubia for nearly five centuries, Egypt slowly declined following the reign of Ramses II. At the New Kingdom's end, Egypt was fragmented into small city-states by power struggles between the pharaohs and the priesthood, and Nubia regained its independence. Many Egyptians also left their country during the crisis, taking refuge in Nubia.

Little is known about Nubia from about 1000 to 850 B.C. By the time Nubia emerges again in the mid-9th century, Napata is its capital and the center

Statues of Ramses II and Queen Nofretari loom over the entrance of the Great Temple of Ramses II at Abu Simbel in Nubia. This temple is the largest of several impressive monuments built by Egyptian pharaohs in the region.

of the state's religious and political power. Ruling the country was a dynasty of Egyptianized kings, aided by a powerful priesthood. The priesthood was centered at Gebel Barkal, a holy mountain site that was the home of Amun, the state god who spoke oracles at his temple and sanctioned the successor to the throne.

The earliest inscriptions dealing with the Napatan dynasty speak of Kashta, who came to rule Egypt in 760 B.C. It is not known precisely how he accomplished this, but scholars speculate that the Egyptian priesthood may have sought the intervention of the Nubian rulers as a means of protection against another threatening power, the Libyans. Kashta accepted the title of pharaoh, legitimizing his authority by making his daughter, Amenirdas I, the divine wife of the god Amun. Kashta returned to Napata, but, when Egypt was later threatened by the Libyans about 730 B.C., his successor, Piankhi (747-716 B.C.), was obliged to provide military assistance.

Piankhi's armies not only defeated the Libyan prince who ruled in northern Egypt but conquered the entire territory. Piankhi had the details of his campaign inscribed on the "Stela of Victory," a commemorative column he installed at the great temple at Gebel Barkal in Napata. (The stela is now preserved in a museum in Cairo.) The inscription on Piankhi's column is one of the most detailed texts of ancient Egypt; the pharaoh describes himself here as raging "like a panther," and descending on his enemy "like a cloudburst." A great lover of horses, Piankhi also told how it pained him to see the poor condition of the king's horses in Egypt. After crushing the enemy, Piankhi left the Egyptians to their own affairs and returned to Napata.

Shabaka (716-702), Piankhi's successor, had to return to Egypt to put down another rebellion in 716 B.C. He remained to set up permanent residence in Egypt, thereby consolidating Nubian jurisdiction over Egypt. Shabaka is therefore regarded as the legitimate founder of what is, in Egyptian history, the 25th dynasty (730-656 B.C.). Whereas Nubia had once been the southern colony of Egypt, Egypt was now the northernmost province of a vast Nubian empire.

5

THE RISE OF MEROË

THE reign of the Nubian pharaohs was a time of Egyptian cultural and economic recovery that lasted for several decades. The Nubians, who were an integral part of Egyptian history, had great admiration for the country's glorious past, and they were inspired to recover its old traditions. For example, they had scribes recopy many of the ancient, worm-eaten religious texts, which were falling apart.

One of the most important of these texts was the Memphite Theology, which the pharaoh Shabaka had permanently recorded on stone. Now in the British Museum in London, the Memphite Theology, also known as the Shabaka Stone, tells the story of the creation of the universe by the god Ptah. It is a highly intellectual account of creation: Ptah first conceived the world in his heart (the source of the intellect), then brought it into being by saying aloud the names of gods, men, temples, and all the other essentials for existence. (This creation theory is quite similar to the opening lines of the Gospel of John in the Bible's New Testament: "In the beginning was the Word, and the Word was with God, and the Word was God.") Under

A stone ram—symbol of the god Amun—kneels before the ruined temples at Naga, one of the main urban centers of Meroitic Nubia.

The Nubian pharaohs became strong supporters of Egyptian tradition, for Nubian history was firmly tied to that of Egypt. This 14th-century B.C. relief fragment depicts Asian and Nubian soldiers in the Egyptian army.

the Nubian pharaohs, Egyptian artists and architects were employed to renovate old temples and build new ones throughout Egypt and Nubia. The religious dedication and good works of the Nubian pharaohs won the support of the Egyptians.

Although the Nubians remained proud of their own heritage, they were willing to adopt Egyptian practices as well. Portraits of Nubian rulers, for example, reveal that the royal dress combined elements from both cultures. One example was the Nubian royal skullcap, which was encircled by a diadem with streamers in the back. Two uraei (representations of sacred asps) were attached to the forehead, symbolizing the kingdoms of Egypt and Nubia. When a Nubian ruler died, his body, like those of the Egyptian pharaohs, was mummified and interred in a pyramid. Succession to the throne, however, was true to Nubian tradition: it was matrilineal, passing to the King's maternal brother or nephew, instead of from father to son, as with the Egyptians.

Taharqa (690–664 B.C.) was the most famous of the Nubian pharaohs. (He is the Ethiopian ruler mentioned in the biblical books of Kings and Esther.) Determined to unify and strengthen the empire, he built many commemorative temples, both in Egypt and in Nubia. Pharaohs traditionally demonstrated their own wealth and power—and thus, the wealth and power of the nation—by constructing temples; Taharqa erected them at Thebes, Tanis, and Edfu in Egypt, as well as at Napata and Kawa in Nubia. He also left numerous stelae describing the high points of his rule. One text reports that, at the beginning of his reign, Taharqa sent for his mother to come from Napata so that she could see him crowned and enjoy the sight of her son as ruler of the two lands.

Taharqa was beset by troubles in his later reign. The Assyrians repeatedly attacked, finally forcing him to withdraw to Nubia in 667 B.C. Tanwetamani (664–653 B.C.), his successor, returned to Egypt and ousted the Assyrians in 664 B.C. However, the next year, Ashurbanipal, the new Assyrian king, attacked and destroyed Egypt with epochal violence. The Assyrians massacred the people in the Egyptian capital of Thebes, sacked the city, and plundered the temples. Tanwetamani fled back to Napata, never to return.

Tanwetamani's defeat effectively ended Nubian rule over Egypt. Nevertheless, the Libyan pharaohs—who had thrown off the Assyrian yoke after the plundering of Thebes and now ruled the north—still considered Nubia a very real threat, and they attacked it in 593 B.C., capturing Napata in the process. The Nubians were now forced to give up all hopes of reclaiming Egypt. Following this disaster, Nubia's history is obscure, but it appears that during the next several centuries, the Nubians gradually moved further south, eventually establishing a new capital at Meroë.

Meroë was situated on the eastern bank of the Nile, about 300 miles south of Napata and roughly halfway between the Fifth and Sixth cataracts. The city became the Nubian kings' chief residence, although Napata remained the nation's primary religious center. Because Meroë was fairly isolated from Egypt and the Mediterranean world, its Nubian population (known as Meroites) developed, over time, a unique and independent civilization—fundamentally African but also containing Hellenistic (late Greek) and Roman cultural elements. This period of ancient Nubia's last great flowering is often called its Golden Age.

After Meroë shifted its interests southward, Nubian influence spread as far as the city of Sennar, situated in today's eastern Sudan. Meroë continued to trade with Egypt (now dominated by the Greek-originated Ptolemy dynasty) as well as with several central African states. Along with gold, copper, precious stones, woods, ivory, and animal skins, the Nubians exported iron objects made by Meroë's busy ironworkers. The average Nubian supported himself by farming and raising cattle.

Meroë included a number of important features. One was Musawwarat es Sufa, a religious center that attracted thousands of pilgrims to its annual festivals honoring the local gods. The Nubians started building Musawwarat around 300 B.C. and, over the next 800 years, continued to add a maze of temples, corridors, and rooms,

many of them dedicated to the local gods. Meroites may have also worshiped the elephant; archaeologists have found the animal's image on numerous artworks and architectural designs at Meroë. Scholars also believe that Musawwarat was the site of an elephant training center, a kind of school where the powerful, intelligent African animals were prepared to take part in military campaigns.

Apedemak, the Meroitic god of war, sun, and abundance, appears in this stone relief, a fragment from the ruins at Naga.

The Meroites worshiped a variety of deities. Among the most important was Apedemak, the god of war, who also symbolized the sun and abundance. Usually depicted wearing armor, Apedemak was represented as a powerful, lion-headed man, sometimes standing aggressively, sometimes sitting regally, and almost always holding lions or elephants on leashes. His muscular hands also gripped weapons of war or, occasionally, prisoners. Apedemak is sometimes portrayed with four arms and three lion heads. Like elephants, lions seem to have been admired by the Meroites as symbols of strength and royal bearing.

Another important sector of Meroë was the vast cemetery complex in the desert east of the city. The common people were buried in graves near the town, the nobility were placed in small pyramids about a mile and a half farther away, and the kings lay in towering pyramids built on ridges yet another three miles away. The Meroitic kings continued this burial tradition until about A.D. 400; more than 40 of their pyramids still exist.

Meroë attained its greatest heights between 90 B.C. and the beginning of the Christian era. Rome, expanding its reach, conquered Egypt between 30 and 28 B.C. The Romans also controlled the Dodekoschoenos, a stretch of the Nile Valley directly below Aswan that was valued because of its gold mines. Attempting to seize this land in about 25 B.C., the Meroites sacked Aswan, Philae, and Elephantine. The Romans retaliated by defeating the Meroites at Napata. Both parties then signed the Treaty of Samos, which established a long period of peace during which Meroë and Roman Egypt enjoyed profitable trade relations. Meroë exported gold, ebony, and ivory, and imported such luxury goods as bronze work, glass, and silverware.

During the 2nd century A.D., the Meroites developed their own alphabet, which they began to use in place of the Egyptian hieroglyphs they had previously employed. A type of shorthand in which the words are separated from one another by dots, the Meroitic script has been studied by scientists for many years. Although they have come to understand the value of the individual letters, the script itself remains undeciphered to this day.

Meroë's craftsmen excelled above all in the creation of fine pottery. This light-colored jar, with its delicate geometric pattern, exemplifies the grace and elegance of Meroitic work.

The arts in Meroë reached a high level of achievement. Blending Egyptian, Greek, and Roman elements, Meroitic artists created their own distinctive style. Sculptors, for example, specialized in carving pairs of statues representing the gods. Doubling as columns, these pieces were placed at the entrances to temples, tombs, and other sacred sites, where they protected the contents from evil. Another distinct category of Meroitic sculpture is the *ba* statue, a concept originating in Egypt. The Egyptians believed that the soul of a dead person became a ba, a bird with a human head, and that these creatures hovered around the deceased person's burial place. The Meroites placed these ba statues outside tombs.

Meroitic craftsmen excelled at making jewelry and pottery, much of which has survived to this day. Using highly sophisticated techniques, jewelers worked in gold, semiprecious stones, and bronze. Their large "shield" rings often bore portraits of the gods or scenes from their lives. Temple carvings of the period show Meroitic rulers wearing these magnificent rings. Beautiful as Meroë's jewelry was, however, it was probably surpassed by the arts of its innovative potters. They fashioned their work either by using a potter's wheel or by shaping their clay by hand. Meroitic pottery produced on the wheel is exceptionally fine and thin. Most of the pottery is painted with elaborate geometric or floral patterns, much of which is original in design. Animal figures—frogs, snakes, crocodiles, giraffes, antelope, and geese—also appear, as do human figures, mythological creatures, and the stars, moon, and Egyptian symbols. Meroitic pottery is probably the finest ever produced in the Nile Valley.

By the 1st century A.D., Meroitic civilization had

reached its peak, and over the next 300 years it experienced gradual decline. Archaeologists base their conviction that Meroë's economy had begun to weaken on the sharp decline in imported goods in the tombs of the period. Axum, the rising kingdom in Abyssinia on the horn of Africa, was now competing with Meroë for the Roman trade. After about A.D. 200, Rome favored trade with Axum because the trade routes through the Red Sea ports were easier and closer to the markets of India, while the overland routes to Meroë had always been difficult and dangerous.

Egypt, which had always been Nubia's major trading partner, was suffering greatly under Roman rule. Nomadic tribesmen from the desert carried on continuous warfare, disrupting commercial activity and everyday life. But although the nomadic warriors had overrun the southern part of the kingdom by the early 4th century, the Meroitic government continued to function. The final blow was not struck until Ezana, Abyssinia's first Christian king, led a military campaign into the region and finally conquered Meroë. Thus ended the glorious empire of one of the ancient world's first great civilizations.

6

A PROCESSION OF FAITHS

WHEN Meroë finally collapsed in A.D. 350, it entered a dark period. The state had been a center for art, architecture, literature, strong government, and religious establishment, but now it seemed to slip beneath the surface of history. For 200 years, between A.D. 350 and 550, no archaeological or written records survived from Meroë.

The extinguishing of Meroë's civilization appears to have been largely the work of a people called the Nobatae. This group had settled in the Meroitic heartland, from Sennar to the Fourth Cataract of the Nile. Archaeologists believe that the Nobatae were poor in material goods; the tumulus graves they left behind reveal limited wealth and isolation from the trading networks of the north.

The northern part of Meroë (Lower Nubia) experienced a smoother transition to a new culture, which scholars have named Ballana, after an important archaeological site. Anthropologists believe that these people were the descendants of the original inhabitants of Meroë, who had mixed with the newcomers, the Nobatae and the Blemmyes. The Nobatae were a

By the 4th century A.D., northern Nubia had developed a new culture, influenced by a mixture of African and Christian traditions. This stone relief of a saint holding a cross conveys the spirit of this post-Meroitic civilization.

89

Nubian-speaking people from the south and west. They became the dominant group during this period; even the Meroitic tongue was eventually replaced with the Nubian language.

The Ballana period seems to have been characterized by the intermingling of strong African traditions, clearly traceable to the earlier Kerma culture, along with the increasing cultural and economic influence of Christian Egypt. African customs are in evidence at the royal tombs of the Nobatae kings buried at Ballana and other sites. The earthen tumuli, numbering about 40, are enormous—as much as 250

This royal crown of silver, inlaid with glass and semiprecious stones, was found in the royal tombs at Ballana in Lower Nubia. The ram's head at the front of the crown, a common emblem of pharaonic Egypt, attests to the extension of Meroitic traditions into the 3rd and 4th centuries A.D.

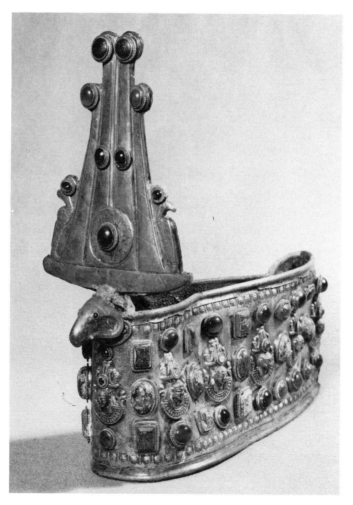

feet wide. They are the wealthiest grave sites in the entire region. The cemeteries were probably linked to administrative centers. Powerful kings controlled different regions, extending their authority throughout Lower Nubia and farther south.

When a king was interred in one of these massive tombs, he was laid out on a wooden bed and adorned with his royal regalia, including silver crowns decorated with glass inlays and semiprecious stones. The royal wife was sacrificed and buried with her husband, as were the king's soldiers and other retainers. Camels, sheep, horses, and other animals were also killed and buried with the king. Horses were interred with all their silver trappings, harnesses, and saddles, in the same way that horses had been buried with the Kushite kings. The horses' grooms accompanied them to the next world. The tombs were well stocked with luxury goods; among them were glassware such as red glass goblets, fine bronze lamps, bronze and silver jewelry, wooden chests, games, rich textiles, pottery, food, wine, and cooking utensils. Some of these items were imported from Egypt, and some were locally manufactured. They attest to the fact that trade with Roman Egypt was significant, and that imports from the Mediterranean were extensive.

Many of the tomb objects suggest the transitional nature of the era. The royal crowns and the tombs themselves continued the traditions of Meroitic culture. The Nobatae kings rejected the pyramid form, returning to the tumulus style that characterized Kerma. The silver crowns exhibit Meroitic motifs derived from pharaonic

Egypt. They utilize the ram's-head symbol, the uraeus (the sacred serpent on Egyptian crowns), the udjat-eye, and the falcon god, Horus.

By the 6th century, three political divisions had emerged in Nubia. The Ballana state became Nobatia, with its capital at Faras; it reached from the First to the Third Cataract. Makuria controlled the region from the Fourth to Fifth Cataracts; Old Dongola was its capital. Farthest south was Alwa, and its capital was Soba, near present-day Khartoum.

In order to strengthen imperial authority, Byzantine policy favored converting the non-Christian peoples who lived along the frontiers of the empire. The kingdom of Axum had adopted Christianity in the 4th century, and the Byzantines intended that the Nubian kingdoms should do the same.

Conversion was complicated, however, by the internal struggles over doctrine within the church. Religious dignitaries argued over two conflicting views: did Jesus have two natures, one divine and one human (the Dyophysite doctrine)? Or did Jesus have a single nature that was solely divine (the Monophysite doctrine)? Byzantine authority supported the Dyophysites, but the Eastern Church espoused the Monophysite viewpoint. Both factions sent missionaries to Nubia, but the Monophysites were more successful. The priest Julian converted the Nobatae in A.D. 543; Makuria, taking a hostile position, chose the orthodox Dyophysite faith. The missionary Longinus converted Alwa to the Monophysite view in A.D. 580. Later, in the 8th century, Makuria would absorb the Nobatae into one great kingdom.

The Nubians' conversion to Christianity served them well. It strengthened their kingdom, giving the king and his subjects a common faith around which to unite. The kings also had at their disposal a literate clergy who encouraged more effective administration.

This 3rd-century Coptic relief represents a Greek motif: the metamorphosis of Daphne.

This newfound unity was put to the test when the Arabs, after conquering Egypt in A.D. 641, tried twice to invade Nubia. The nation's resistance, spearheaded by the famous Nubian archers, was so strong that both sides agreed to a compromise. In 652, they signed a treaty that guaranteed Nubian independence in return for an annual tribute of 360 slaves and the maintenance of a mosque that had been built at Old Dongola: this peace lasted for 600 years.

The next two centuries were a time of prosperity and growth for the Nubian states. The new religion brought fundamental change: church and state were separated, and the administration of the legal system was made more efficient. No longer regarded as divine, the king now had little control over his people's personal religious affairs. This ended the royal burial of kings as a symbol of their power; there were no tombs built for Christian kings in Nubia. And although the king was still technically an absolute ruler,

The ruins at Faras, the capital of Nobatia, offer evidence of Christian Nubia's aesthetic achievements. This stone relief was uncovered during excavations of Faras in the early 1960s.

he no longer had unquestioned authority over the people.

The king's second in command, the *eparch*, was a kind of viceroy, responsible for maintaining trade relations with Moslem Egypt and for protecting Nubia's northern frontier. Egyptian Moslems were allowed to enter the country to trade and to settle in the north (Lower Nubia). As a safety measure against Islamic influence, however, the Moslems were forbidden to go beyond the Second Cataract without Nubian permission.

Faras Cathedral was one of the most impressive religious structures in Nubia, especially celebrated for the 169 murals that decorated its walls. These murals, considered the masterpieces of Nubian art, were painted in the church interiors beginning in the 8th century. They show Byzantine and Coptic influences, but the brilliant, bold use of colors seems unmistakably Nubian. Among the paintings' subjects were the Madonna, the Crucifixion, and the Nativity. Artists also painted portraits of Nubian kings, eparchs, and bishops, with identifying inscriptions. (Excavated by the Polish Archaeological Mission from 1961 to 1964, the Faras murals are now divided between the National Museum in Warsaw, Poland, and the National Museum of Antiquities in Khartoum.)

By the Middle Ages, the religious spirit in Nubia, as in Europe, seemed to give way to military concerns. After the 12th century, church building was replaced by the construction of elaborate, fortified castles. Both the influence of the Christian church and that of the rulers were waning. The monarchs were weakened by internal fighting and challenges from local warlords. The tensions and conflicts caused dislocation as people left Lower Nubia, moving south for safety. Local industries and commercial activity steadily declined. Finally, in the late 14th century, the powerful kingdoms disintegrated into warring principalities. They were now open to invasions by Arab nomads and conquerors from Islamic Egypt. After 10 centuries of Christianity, Nubians became followers of Islam, and they remain so to this day.

7

THE ANCIENT KINGDOM OF AXUM

ANCIENT Axum was a powerful kingdom that extended its domination over the horn of Africa and southern Arabia. The Axumites developed a complex political state, advanced agricultural methods, and a vigorous trade with the rest of Africa, the Middle East, and India. They erected large-scale monuments, developed their own written language, adopted Christianity, and left to posterity one of history's most compelling legends, the story of the queen of Sheba.

Ancient Axum is known today as Ethiopia, a Greek-rooted word meaning "land of the sun-burned [or black-faced] men." The term first appears in writing in the *Iliad* and *Odyssey* of Homer, the great classical Greek poet. The name *Ethiopia* was soon widely adopted to refer to the country of the dark-skinned peoples of Africa and Asia. The actual residents of the land, however, did not call it Ethiopia. Their name for the land came from a source far more ancient.

The architects of the ancient empire of Axum excelled in the construction of giant stelae. The largest of these, designed to stand 110 feet high, now lies in ruins.

Cool, dry highlands dominate the Ethiopian landscape near Axum. This area was once inhabited by a Kushitic-speaking people who traded with the residents of Egypt, Meroë, and Arabia.

The territory that was to become the Axumite kingdom lay to the east and south of the upper Nile River, rising in a massive range of mountains extend-

ing from the Blue Nile to the Red Sea. The East
African Rift Valley divides the mountains, whose
awesome peaks and deep clefts protected the ancient

land from outside invasions. The northern area is a region of cool, dry highlands; conversely, the climate of the southern lowlands is tropical.

The original inhabitants of the northern highlands spoke Kushitic languages. Developers of one of the earliest agricultural centers in Africa, they used a form of plow to raise such crops as wheat and barley, which came from Egypt, and teff, a native grain. The Kushitic highlanders had long-standing relationships with the peoples of Egypt, Meroë, and Arabia. A thousand years before the Christian era, southern Arabians began crossing the Red Sea to trade with and settle among the indigenous peoples. There were probably many groups, but surviving inscriptions mention only the Sabeans, the Agazians, and the Habasha.

With them, these peoples brought their languages and skills in architecture and agriculture. The southern Arabians were knowledgeable in quarrying and transporting stone. They were also adept at constructing large buildings, producing stone sculpture, and cutting inscriptions. The northeast Africans and the southern Arabians traveled back and forth, sharing their cultures between them. The Kushitic and Sabean tongues combined to form Ge'ez, Ethiopia's classical language. *Agazian* and *Habasha* were apparently terms that the ancient Ethiopians used for themselves. Some scholars have linked *Agazian* to the word *Ge'ez*, and from *Habasha* has come the English variant *Abyssinia*, until the 20th century the most common name for the country in European sources. Out of this culture-sharing between Africans and Arabians emerged the kingdom of Axum.

The Axumites established their kingdom on the northeastern highland plateau during the 1st century A.D. This was an advantageous position in terms of trade. It was to Adulis, its major port, that Africans from the interior brought iron, animal hides, ivory,

slaves, gold, tortoiseshell, and spices to exchange for practical and luxury goods. Ptolemy, the 2nd-century mathematician and geographer, made the first known reference to Axum: in his naval and merchant guide, *Circumnavigation of the Erythrean Sea*, Ptolemy wrote about a people called Axumites and about their port, Adulis, which was the center of the ivory trade.

Although the origins of Axum remain obscure, archaeological records trace its roots to a highly developed pre-Christian culture. This limestone sculpture from a site near the city of Axum dates back to the 5th century B.C.

Axum reached its height in the mid-4th century under the rule of Ezana, a strong king whose successful military campaigns secured the nation's trade routes by land and sea. Ezana attacked and plundered Meroë in A.D. 330, carrying off many prisoners and much livestock. As a result of his successes, Axum gained control over the northeast caravan routes in Nubia. The king then extended his authority over southern Arabia (now called Yemen) and the Beja, the nomads who traversed the deserts surrounding Axum. Ezana now controlled the Red Sea trade and was part of a commercial network that linked the Mediterranean, the East African coast, and the Middle East with the markets of India. During the 3rd century, Axum also began to mint its own gold, silver, and copper coins, an indication of its significant participation in international trade.

King Ezana's reign is extremely important because he established Christianity as the official religion in Axum. Today in Ethiopia it is widely believed that Christianity was brought to the country by the apostle Philip. This belief is based upon the New Testament (Acts 8:26–39), where it is said that Philip met an Ethiopian who was a treasurer under Candace, queen of the Ethiopians. Philip baptized the treasurer, who is thought to have been the first person to preach Christianity in Ethiopia.

Because classical writers used *Ethiopian* as a term to identify all dark-skinned peoples, it is almost impossible to determine if the reference in Acts actually refers to the more limited region of modern-day Ethiopia. In addition, *Candace* was a term used as the title of the queen mother of Meroë. A number of scholars therefore attribute the passage to the Nubians, rather than the Axumites. At any rate, the Nubians and the Axumites were Ethiopians as far as the classical world was concerned. Perhaps the biblical text may best be understood as referring generally to the spread of Christianity and its acceptance by ancient Africans.

A clearer record, however, does exist in the Ethiopian tradition and in the records of church historians. According to these sources, Christianity was brought to Axum by Frumentius, a Syrian youth who was traveling to India. At the time, relations between foreign merchants and the Axumite government were hostile, and Frumentius's ship was attacked when it reached Axum. Everyone aboard was killed except the boy, perhaps because he was so young.

Frumentius was brought as a slave to the court of Alla Ameida, Ezana's father; there, he soon became the king's treasurer and tutor to the royal children. Alla Ameida died in A.D. 325, but not before promising Frumentius his freedom. But the queen, now acting as regent until her young sons, Ezana and Shaiazana, could take the throne, asked Frumentius to remain and help govern the country.

Frumentius stayed for another three years, during which time he quietly provided places for Christians to worship. Most Axumites still practiced the traditional religions, but many people were familiar with Christian ideals and practices; Axum, like Nubia, had served as a place of refuge for persecuted Christians fleeing Egypt, Syria, and other parts of the eastern Roman empire. After Ezana and Shaiazana were enthroned in A.D. 328, Frumentius traveled to Egypt. There he visited Athanasius, bishop of Alexandria, and told him about the Axumite royal family's favor-

This 80-foot obelisk—the tallest of the intact Axumite stelae—is carved to resemble a 10-story building, with a door at its base and windows on every floor.

able attitude toward Christianity. Before long, Athanasius consecrated Frumentius bishop of the Axumite church and sent him back to Axum. Sometime around 336, Frumentius returned to Axum, where he was warmly received.

Ezana and Shaiazana were still loyal to the old gods, but they nevertheless permitted Frumentius to spread his faith in Axum. Before long, they, too, converted to Christianity. Ezana took the baptismal name of Abraham, and Shaiazana, that of Atsbaha.

Scholars have suggested that the court at Axum was willing to convert because of its close relationship with Byzantium, then ruled by the Roman emperor known as Constantine the Great. Axum and Byzantium (present-day Turkey) shared significant cultural and commercial interests. Byzantium's splendor and power, along with the spread of Christianity at its court, certainly influenced Axum's royal family. Axum's acceptance of the new religion was a political as well as a religious decision, for it fostered good relations with Constantine and cemented Axum's position as the cultural and commercial center of northeast Africa.

The Axumite church, because of its connections to Alexandria, followed the Copts, or Egyptian Christians, in adhering to the Monophysite doctrine (which held that Christ had one nature, which was the same as that of God). Other Christians believed in the two natures of Christ, the divine and the human. When the Monophysite doctrine won out in the Council of Chalcedon (A.D. 450), Egypt and Axum split from the Constantinople Church and the Church of Rome, and formed the Coptic Church of Egypt and the Ethiopian Orthodox Church.

Numerous Monophysite Christians sought refuge in Axum. Some of them were missionaries who paved the way for Christianity's growth in the country. In about 502, a group of evangelists known as the Nine Saints immigrated to Axum; there they lived and

taught in various places, and churches and convents
grew up around them. They often built new churches
on the sites of pre-Christian temples, which encouraged the local people to adopt Christianity because
their ancient places of worship continued to be respected. People made pilgrimages to these holy sites.
Christianity was also spread by hundreds of native and
foreign monks.

The religious communities or monasteries were
initially supported by the surrounding villages, but
they soon received huge land grants from the Axumite
kings as well. King Gabre Maskal began this policy in
the 6th century with the monastery of Debra Damo.
Subsequent kings followed suit, making the church a
wealthy, land-owning institution. In the future, and
through the history of the country, the church would
frequently challenge the power of the kings.

Ezana was the greatest king of the Axumite era,
not only for his military exploits and for making Axum
a Christian state, but for his reputation as an important patron of the arts. As king, he sponsored the
building of large-scale monuments in Axum, a policy
already observed in the other Nile Valley civilizations
of Egypt and Nubia.

Like their neighbors, Axumite craftsmen likewise
created their own unique style of architecture. Monument construction on a grand scale was expressed in
giant stelae, churches, and royal palaces. Axumite
architecture was characterized by the use of stone and
a square or rectangular layout. Usually, the buildings
were several stories high and included basements.
Wood was used for the frames of doorways and windows, in the roofs, and in the beams that supported
the floors in upper-story constructions.

**The grand stelae at Axum remain the most
famous monuments of the era. These elegant, tall
stones were carefully finished and decorated to**

resemble multiple-storied buildings. Stelae exist at other sites around Axum, but none are as magnificent. Architects normally built them in groups. The tallest of the obelisks still standing is nearly 80 feet tall (including the 9 feet sunk into the ground). It was gracefully carved to look like a 10-story edifice; its base is a replica of a false door. The largest obelisk, however, today lies broken in pieces on the ground. One hundred and ten feet high and carved to imitate a 13-story building, it probably toppled during construction. Archaeologists believe the stelae originally marked grave sites. Extensive underground tombs have been excavated nearby, and stone sarcophagi have been found in the burial chambers.

Matara, lying halfway between Axum and the port of Adulis, was another important city. Excavations show that it was clearly a key urban center of economic and political importance. The site includes churches, tombs, and residential areas. The average home had one to three rooms. Archaeologists have found gold work of Roman origin, a sure indication of the wealth of some of Matara's citizens.

The introduction of Christianity had a profound impact upon the growth of Axumite literature. Previously, the Greek language dominated because of Axum's ties to the Hellenistic world. But after Christianity was introduced, Ge'ez, the native tongue, became the national language. The most important literary achievement of the era was the translation of the Bible into Ge'ez, which took place from the 4th century to the early 7th century. The Nine Saints began the translation of the Old Testament, using the Greek version of the Bible called the Septuagint. All of the canonical and apocryphal books make up the Ethiopian Bible, as well as some pseudepigrapha

Even after the demise of the Axumite empire, the Christian tradition lived on in Ethiopia. Its legacy can be seen in this 18th-century painting of the Madonna and child from Gondar, some 150 miles southwest of Axum.

(anonymous religious writing, such as the Psalms of Solomon). The Bible, as it came into use in Axum, assumed the utmost importance, becoming the basis for all literary and religious expression. Because few other Western works were available, the Bible was even regarded as the source of science and philosophy.

The legend of Solomon and Sheba, for centuries a favorite in Arabia and North Africa, is indissolubly

linked to Ethiopian literature. Ethiopia's close relationship with southern Arabia, specifically the country of Yemen, strengthens its claim on the legend even
more. The main literary source for the Ethiopian
version is the *Kebra Nagast* (The History of the Kings),
a collection of legends and traditions beloved by the
Ethiopians. But although the book was not compiled
until the 14th century, the Sheba legend had been
widely known in the country since the early 7th
century. The story is a liberally embellished version of
the biblical narrative in 1 Kings 10:1–13. It also
borrows from the Muslims' Koran, apocryphal literature, and other ancient Coptic and Arabic sources.
The story's appeal seems ageless:

Once, a certain wise man and merchant named
Tamrin journeyed from the nation of Sheba to the
kingdom of Solomon to see the magnificent sights and
hear the king's famed wisdom. When Tamrin returned
to his country, he told Makeda, the queen of Sheba,
of the wondrous things he had witnessed and of
Solomon's uncommon wisdom. Impressed, the queen
decided to visit Solomon's kingdom herself. Makeda
arrived in Jerusalem with gifts for the king: precious
stones, spices, and gold. Solomon received her visit
and gifts most gladly and presented her with many
fine presents in return. She tested his wisdom with
ingenious questions, which Solomon grasped and an-
swered with ease. The queen planned to spend six
months at King Solomon's beautiful palace, then return to her own country.

But Solomon fell in love with the queen and
planned a trick that would enable him to sleep with
her. After an evening of feasting, he told her that she
would be free to return home if, during the night, she
partook of nothing that belonged to him. But the king
had heavily spiced the food, and during the night the
queen reached for water to quench her thirst. Watch-
ing her, Solomon caught her in the act and completed
the bargain by spending the night with her. Later that
night, Solomon dreamed of a brilliant sun shining

over both his land and that of the queen. He interpreted this as a sign that Makeda would bear his child. Before the queen left for home, he gave her a ring and said that if she bore a male child, that child should come to Jerusalem, identifying himself with the ring.

> It came to pass that the queen did bear a male child, whom she named Menelik. When he grew up, Menelik went to visit his father, Solomon, who tried to persuade him to stay in Jerusalem, site of the house of God and his tabernacle. Menelik, however, not only returned to his country but stole the ark of the covenant from the tabernacle. The ark, an elaborate chest representing the supreme deity, was the most sacred object of the Jewish faith. With the ark, Menelik brought Judaism to the land of Sheba, where today many Ethiopians continue to practice that faith, now called Falasha. Many modern-day Ethiopians firmly believe that the dynasty started by Menelik I began with the queen of Sheba in Ethiopia and King Solomon in Jerusalem. This may be historical fiction, but it points to the actual African-Asiatic heritage of the Ethiopians.

King Ezana had carried Axum to its highest level of achievement. He was followed, however, by far less capable rulers, resulting in about 150 years of national decline. But at the beginning of the 6th century, the emperor Caleb ascended the throne, and Axum experienced another high point in its history. It began with the emperor's defense of Christianity, a move that Caleb had to make because of his people's commitment to that religion and because powerful neighboring Byzantium demanded it.

Two fiercely competing religions—Christianity

and Judaism—had taken root in South Arabia (to-day's Yemen). After choosing Judaism, the local prince, Joseph, launched a campaign of aggressive persecution against all Christians, including Axum-ites who lived in his domain. In A.D. 523, he began his campaign in Zafar, a largely Christian city guarded by a garrison of about 300 Axumite soldiers. To clear the way for conquest, Joseph tricked the soldiers; he promised that if they surrendered and spent the night in his camp, he would allow them to return to Axum unharmed. When the unsuspecting soldiers were asleep, however, Joseph ordered his men to fall on them and cut off their heads.

As soon as Joseph gained entry into the town he sealed up the churches and set them on fire. Many Christians inside, young men and women, old people, and children, were burned alive. Joseph ordered oth-ers to renounce Christianity or prepare to die. Some complied under force, while others became martyrs rather than give up their faith. Joseph threatened to burn the homes and take the property of any Jews found hiding or protecting Christians.

Joseph carried out the same aggressive policy throughout southern Arabia. The infamous massacre of Christians in the town of Nagran finally impelled the other Christian emperors to act. Justin I, the emperor of Byzantium, asked Caleb, as the nearest Christian ruler, to avenge the murder of the Chris-tians. Caleb launched a full-scale campaign in A.D. 525, successfully assaulting southern Arabia; Joseph died in the conflict.

Axum was again the most powerful empire in the Red Sea region, but its glory was brief. Caleb had appointed a governor to rule over southern Arabia, but he was overthrown by a certain Abreha. Abreha agreed to pay tribute to Axum, but he otherwise ruled southern Arabia independently. He built a grand ca-thedral at San'a and, in A.D. 570, sent an expedition

to Mecca to destroy the Ka'ba. In this mission, he
failed. Although his soldiers were equipped with many
mighty elephants, their advance was halted on the
outskirts of Mecca when a plague broke out and killed
most of the men.

Axumite colonization in southern Arabia finally
ended at the close of the 6th century, when the area
was overrun by the Persians. Bitterly opposed to
Christianity, the Persians favored those religious
groups that were also hostile to the religion. The loss
of its colonies in southern Arabia weakened Axum's
international prestige: Byzantium seems to have broken off its ties to Axum at this time. Furthermore, the
Persians disrupted the trade routes in the Red Sea
area. Persian rule was short-lived, however. All Arabia and North Africa soon fell under the onslaught of
Islam. The spread of a new faith helped to cut off
Axum from South Arabia and its spiritual head, the
Patriarch of Alexandria in Egypt, as well as from its
crucial trade with the Greco-Byzantine world. Axum's
position as the major power in northeast Africa and
the Red Sea region was no more.

During the 8th century, Axum lost much of its
northern territory to the encroaching Beja (Muslim
nomads). Islam was also spreading among the ethnic
groups along the east African coast. In response, the
Axumites started to move, and to conquer peoples and
territory farther south. They were largely successful,
reestablishing their trade links with South Arabia and
reconquering some of their territory along the coastal
strip.

In the 970s, the Agaw, a non-Christian ethnic
group headed by Queen Judith, wreaked havoc upon
the Axumites. Intent on overthrowing their powerful
neighbor, the Agaw destroyed property, burned
countless churches, and killed most of the royal family. Axum finally forced Queen Judith and her army
to withdraw, but by then the Axumites were so ex-

hausted spiritually and physically that they lacked the energy to rebuild their kingdom.

The civilization would survive, but the future center of power in Ethiopia was destined to be the south. The Axumites retired to their mountainous strongholds in the north. So ended the Axumite era in Ethiopia, the last of the magnificent ancient empires of northeast Africa.

FURTHER READING

Adams, William. *Nubia, Corridor to Africa*. Princeton, NJ: Princeton University Press, 1977.

Cambridge Ancient History. Vol. 1–3. Rev. ed. Cambridge: Cambridge University Press, 1970–82.

Levine, Donald. *Greater Ethiopia: The Evolution of a Multi-ethnic Society*. Chicago: University of Chicago Press, 1974.

Mokhtar, G., ed. *General History of Africa*. Vol. 2. Berkeley: University of California Press, 1990.

Stead, Miriam. *Egyptian Life*. London: British Museum Publications, 1986.

Taylor, John. *Egypt and Nubia*. Cambridge: Harvard University Press, 1991.

Ullendorff, Edward. *The Ethiopians: An Introduction to Country and People*. London: Oxford University Press, 1960.

Wenig, Steffen. *Africa in Antiquity: The Arts of Ancient Nubia and the Sudan*. 2 vols. New York: Brooklyn Museum, 1978.

Wilson, J. *The Culture of Ancient Egypt*. Chicago: University of Chicago Press, 1975.

INDEX

Abu Simbel, Nubia, 74
Abyssinia, 87, 100. *See also* Axum
Admonitions of a Sage (Ipu-wer), 20
Adulis, Axum, 100, 101, 107
Africa, 19, 25, 26, 100
Ahmose I (pharaoh of Egypt), 25, 73
Akhenaton (pharaoh of Egypt), 28.
Alexander the Great, 32, 33
Alla Ameida (king of Axum), 103
Amenemhet I (pharaoh of Egypt), 23, 71
Amenemhet III (pharaoh of Egypt), 24
Amenemhet IV (pharaoh of Egypt), 24
Amenhotep I (pharaoh of Egypt), 25, 32
Amenhotep II (pharaoh of Egypt), 27, 32
Amenhotep III (pharaoh of Egypt), 27–28, 29, 64, 74
Amenhotep IV. *See* Akhenaton
Amon-Ra (Egyptian god), 23, 28, 31, 33, 45, 46, 74
Amun (Nubian god), 76
Apedemak (Meroite god), 84

Arabia, 97, 100, 102, 108, 109, 111, 112
Assyrians, 29, 33, 81
Athanasius, 103–4
Aton (Egyptian god), 28
Atum (Egyptian god), 37
Axum, 87, 92, 97–113
art, 106–7

Ballana culture, 89, 90, 92
Blemmyes, the, 89

Caleb (king of Axum), 110–11
Chalcedon, Council of, 105
Christianity, 84, 87, 90, 92, 93, 95, 97, 100, 103–6, 107, 111, 112
Circumnavigation of the Erythrean Sea (Ptolemy), 101
Coptic, 95, 105, 109

Djoser (pharaoh of Egypt), 15
Djoser, stepped pyramid of, 15
Dyophysite doctrine, 92, 105

Egypt, ancient, 13–67, 69, 81, 82, 84, 87, 90, 91, 92, 93, 94, 95, 100, 106, 112
art, 15, 16–17, 25–26,

27, 28, 33, 53, 56, 73, 76, 77, 80
daily life, 51–67
Lower, 13, 19, 22–23, 24, 30, 31
Nubian occupation, 70–75
religion, 15, 23, 35–49
Upper, 13, 21–22, 31, 33
Ethiopia, 97, 102, 109, 113
Ethiopian Orthodox Church, 105
Ezana (king of Axum), 87, 102–3, 105, 106, 110

Faras Cathedral, 94–95
Frumentius, 103–5

Gabre Maskal (king of Axum), 106
Geb (Egyptian god), 38
Gebel Barkal, Nubia, 76
Giza pyramids, 16–17, 18, 57
Ge'ez language, 100, 107

Habasha, the, 100
Hatshepsut (queen of Egypt), 25–26
Hattusilis (king of the Hittites), 29
Heliopolis, Egypt, 18, 37, 45
Heri-Hor, 31
Hiracleopolis, Egypt, 22
Hittites, 29

Horemheb (pharaoh of
Egypt), 28–29
Horus (Egyptian god), 38,
40, 41, 42, 48, 92
Hyksos, the, 24–25, 45

Imhotep, 15
Ineb-Hedj, Egypt, 14. *See
also* Memphis
Intermediate Period
First, 19–22
Second, 24–25
Third, 31–33, 61
Ipu-wer, 20
Isis (Egyptian goddess),
38–41, 51
Islam, 94, 95, 109, 112

Judaism, 110, 111
Julian, 92

Kadesh, Battle of, 29
Kashta (king of Nubia), 76
Kebra Nagast (The History
of the Kings), 109
Kerma, Nubia, 71, 73, 90,
91
Khafra (pharaoh of
Egypt), 16
Khufu (pharaoh of Egypt),
16

Libya, 30
Libyans, 15, 19, 31, 32,
76, 81
Longinus, 92

Memphis, Egypt, 13, 14,
18, 45
Memphite Theology,
45–46, 79

Menes (pharaoh of
Egypt), 13, 14
Menkhare (pharaoh of
Egypt), 16
Mentuhotep II (pharaoh
of Egypt), 23
Meroë, 79–87, 89, 90,
100, 102
alphabet, 84–85
art, 86, 89, 91, 92
religion, 82–84
Middle Kingdom, 22–24,
55, 58
Mitannians, the, 27
Monophysite doctrine, 92,
105
Musawwarat es Sufa,
82–83
Mutawallis (king of the
Hittites), 29
Mutemwiya (queen of
Egypt), 27

Napata, Nubia, 74, 76, 81,
82, 84
Napatan dynasty, 76
Nephtys (Egyptian
goddess), 38
New Kingdom, 25–31,
45–47, 55, 60, 61, 73, 74
Nile Delta, 22, 25, 29, 31,
33
Nile River, 13, 23, 25, 40,
44, 69, 70, 71, 74, 82,
89, 98
Nile Valley, 19, 57, 65,
84, 86, 106
Nine Saints, the, 105, 107
Nobatae, the, 89, 90, 91
Nubia, 19, 23–24, 25, 28,
29, 31, 69–82, 87, 89,
90, 91, 94, 95, 102, 106.

See also Meroë
art, 70, 73, 95
Christianity, conversion
to, 92, 93, 103
Egyptian occupation,
76–81
Nubian pharaohs, 76,
79, 80
Nut (Egyptian goddess), 38

Old Kingdom, 15–19
Osiris (Egyptian god), 23,
38–41, 45, 51

Palestine, 19, 25, 27, 29,
31, 32
Pa-Ramses (pharaoh of
Egypt), 29
Pepy I (pharaoh of Egypt),
14, 19
Pepy II (pharaoh of
Egypt), 19
Persians, 33, 112
Piankhi (king of Nubia),
76
Ptah (Egyptian god), 15,
45, 74, 79
Punt, 19, 25

Ra (Egyptian god), 18, 45,
64. *See also* Amon-Ra
Ramses II (pharaoh of
Egypt), 28, 29, 32, 74
Ramses III (pharaoh of
Egypt), 30–31, 32
Ramses IV (pharaoh of
Egypt), 31
Ramses IX (pharaoh of
Egypt), 31
Red Sea, 99, 100, 102,
111, 112

Saite dynasty, 33
Samos, Treaty of, 84
Semenkhka-ra (pharaoh of Egypt), 28
Sensuret I (pharaoh of Egypt), 23
Sensuret III (pharaoh of Egypt), 23–24
Seth (Egyptian god), 38–40, 48
Sethnakhr (pharaoh of Egypt), 30
Seti I (pharaoh of Egypt), 29, 32
Shabaka (king of Nubia), 77, 79
Shaiazana (king of Axum), 103, 105
Sheba, queen of, 97, 108
    legend of, 109–10

Sheshonq I (pharaoh of Egypt), 32
Shu (Egyptian god), 38
Snefru (pharaoh of Egypt), 15, 16, 70
Sobek Neferu (queen of Egypt), 24
Solomon (king of Jerusalem), 32, 108–10
Somalia, 19
Sudan, 25, 69, 82
Syria, 19, 25, 27, 29, 31, 33, 103

Taharqa (king of Nubia), 81
Tanwetamani (king of Nubia), 81
Thebes, Egypt, 22, 23, 25, 26, 28, 29, 31, 32, 45, 46, 60, 61, 81
Thoth (Egyptian god), 40, 41–42
Thutmose I (pharaoh of Egypt), 25, 27
Thutmose II (pharaoh of Egypt), 25
Thutmose III (pharaoh of Egypt), 25–27, 32
Thutmose IV (pharaoh of Egypt), 27
Tutankhamen (pharaoh of Egypt), 28

Unis (pharaoh of Egypt), 18

Valley of the Kings, 28, 47, 60

Yemen, 102, 109, 111

PICTURE CREDITS

EARNESTINE JENKINS holds a master's degree in art history (specializing in Egypt and Nubia) and is currently working toward her Ph.D. at Michigan State University. In 1985 she spent several months in Egypt with an archaeological team from the British Exploration Society, and in 1990 and 1991 she lived in Ethiopia, where she studied that nation's ancient language, Ge'ez. After completing her doctoral dissertation, entitled "Popular Religion in Ethiopia," Jenkins plans to teach history and art.

CLAYBORNE CARSON, senior consulting editor of the MILESTONES IN BLACK AMERICAN HISTORY series, is a professor of history at Stanford University. His first book, *In Struggle: SNCC and the Black Awakening of the 1960s* (1981), won the Frederick Jackson Turner Prize of the Organization of American Historians. He is the director of the Martin Luther King, Jr., Papers Project, which will publish 12 volumes of King's writings.

DARLENE CLARK HINE, senior consulting editor of the MILESTONES IN BLACK AMERICAN HISTORY series, is the John A. Hannah Professor of American History at Michigan State University. She is the author of numerous books and articles on black women's history. Her most recent work is the two-volume *Black Women in America: An Historical Encyclopedia* (1993).